Caroline Wells Healey Dall

Egypts Place in History

Caroline Wells Healey Dall

Egypts Place in History

ISBN/EAN: 9783337330415

Printed in Europe, USA, Canada, Australia, Japan

Cover: Foto ©ninafisch / pixelio.de

More available books at **www.hansebooks.com**

Price of this Pamphlet, $1.50.   Price of the Original Work, $70.00.

Egypt's Place in History.

A PRESENTATION.

By MRS. DALL.

"Altera manu fert lapidem, altera panem ostentat." — PLAUTUS.

"O mihi tam longæ maneat pars ultima vitæ,
  Spiritus. et quantum sat erit tua discere facta!" — VIRGIL.

BOSTON:
LEE AND SHEPARD.
1868.

EGYPT'S PLACE IN HISTORY.

'S PLACE IN HISTORY.

A PRESENTATION.

By MRS. DALL.

"Altera manu fert lapidem, altera panem ostentat." — PLAUTUS.

"O mihi tam longæ maneat pars ultima vitæ,
 Spiritus, et quantum sat erit tua discere facta!" — VIRGIL.

BOSTON:
LEE AND SHEPARD.
1868.

Egypt's Place in History.

A PRESENTATION.

By MRS. DALL.

"Altera manu fert lapidem, altera panem ostentat." — PLAUTUS.

"O mihi tam longæ maneat pars ultima vitæ,
  Spiritus, et quantum sat erit tua discere facta!" — VIRGIL.

BOSTON:
LEE AND SHEPARD.
1868.

Entered according to Act of Congress, in the year 1868, by
MRS. DALL,
In the Clerk's Office of the District Court of the District of Massachusetts.

CAMBRIDGE:
PRESS OF JOHN WILSON AND SON.

PREFACE.

"YOUR work is not finished," wrote Bunsen once to Max Müller, "when you have brought the ore from the mine. It must be sifted, smelted, refined, and coined, before it can be of real use, and contribute to the well-being of mankind." These words confront me with their discouragement, as I send away the last proofs of this pamphlet. Yet I think, if Bunsen were here, he would appreciate the motive which makes me risk the mortification which may come from obvious incompetency, and persist in sending these sheets through the press.

If there were, in this country, a single periodical which would consent to publish one or two *representative* articles in every issue, there would never have been any need of this publication. Papers, of a kind which have given to Sainte Beuve a European reputation, have no acceptance here. Theological Reviews want brief summaries, or the wretched dogmatisms of nameless critics. Even the "North-American" prefers the theories and conclusions of our own scholars, to a clear *resumé* of the labors of the best foreign students. To my mind, the *resumé* is more useful than the criticism; for I like to judge things for myself, and am not very grateful to men who retouch masterpieces before they exhibit them.

It is not enough to say, that there is no scholar in America capable of criticising every department of Bunsen's work. There is no such man in Europe; and my late correspondence with scientific men, in reference to the matters here brought out, shows me that those who worked for him worked each in his own line, without the least idea to what their united labors were tending. It was left to Bunsen to harmonize the materials, and show the bearing of the facts on each other, and on his own theories.

Neither Dr. Birch nor Lepsius could tell me what prompted Bunsen to use the eccentric period of 21,000 years, instead of the universally accepted 25,000, to designate what he calls the nutation of the ecliptic. I do not present the conclusions of Bunsen to the public, because I am sure that they are all sound, because I am prepared to defend them right and left, or because I believe that none of them will ever be impugned. In the main bearing of his chronological scheme, I have perfect faith; yet that many a side-prop will perish, I think, is very likely. But we never can have grand and thorough investigation, until some one disregards prudence, and risks collateral failure. No one understood this better than Bunsen himself. When he threw his great bridge of thought across the ages, a pier was often needed, for which the past had provided no solid support. Upon any *tenacious* foundation, were it only of mud and straw, our scholar was willing to erect a temporary structure, quite sure, that, after the arch was once projected, the continuous framework would hold it firmly in its place; and the perishable material might be gradually and safely replaced, at need, from the quarries of the future.

What I especially value in Bunsen is his estimate of the work necessary to be done, before we can decide the age of man, of history, and of revelation.

The special boon which will be conferred upon theological students, by a familiarity with his conclusions, is just a little — modesty!

They will understand better what their own speculations involve: they will hesitate, before adding another to the stupid dogmatisms of the world. They will find in him a sincere reverence for God and Truth. They will see how all theories and superstitions sink into insignificance before the actual facts. They will see that every year clears up mysteries, presents discrepancies, and annihilates dreams. Above all, they will perceive that the most truly religious man of his time, Bunsen was also the only man, so far, to suspect the breadth and depth of the preparatory work to be done in Scriptural Interpretation. There is genius in the mere conception of such toil as he has undergone, — something godlike in the sustained strength and insight with which it was carried through.

But if he knew how to deal with "weightiest matters of the law," he knew also how to throw an infinite charm about all literary subjects. The personal enthusiasm which the man created in his lifetime was something extraordinary. One of the earliest impressions made upon me, in childhood, was of the tumult of love and wonder excited in American travellers, by interviews with him they called "The Chevalier," while he was still unknown and young. In Switzerland and England, no less than in Rome, he was the delight of all who met him, — a feeling Dean Stanley has well expressed in his recent Preface to the English translation of Bunsen's "God in History." "How thrilling," he says, "was the moment in which I first saw the beloved friend of Arnold, of whose gifts and graces we had been taught to expect so much! How rare a sight were those singular re-unions of all that was most distinguished in London society! There was to be met the young Sanscrit scholar,* introduced to the English world under his fostering care, to accomplish the mighty work of editing the Veda, and stimulated by the same genial encouragement to give us also the precious fragments and chips of his German workshop. There was more than one rising and wayward genius, then lingering in the outer courts of the church or world, who seemed, in the sight of that benevolent and beaming countenance, to understand how devils could, by a mere look, be cast out, and flee away. There was the ever-flowing fountain of knowledge, old and new; the story of many a stirring incident in foreign lands; the anticipation of many a prospect, bright or dark, which coming events have reached."

Any one might be proud to have *the right* to introduce this man and his work to popular regard. *I* do it only because it is impossible to understand modern Biblical criticism, without some knowledge of his labors and services; and because it is customary to find them denounced and misrepresented in most unexpected quarters.

If this small edition of my pamphlet should lead to another and larger, I shall add to it a table of all the kings of Egypt, from Menes to the last Sebennyte, in chronological order, with their individual relations to the monuments of the country, and general history, briefly expressed. I have prepared it for my own use; but it seems absurd to print it, unless some demand should arise.

* Professor Max Müller.

PREFACE.

I have taken no liberties with Bunsen. When I express my own opinion, or explain his mysteries, or follow up his illustrations, I think I have always made my share in the matter clear.

By carefully working out his projections, I have altered some misprinted numerals in his tables, which disfigure his own book, and perplexed me for months.

In the table of "Dispersion," on the sixty-ninth page, I have risked the insertion of Mts. as an abbreviation for "mountains" (near Lebanon), in the place of *Mas*, which stands in his own table, and which no one has ever ventured to explain.

When he asserts, that, "since the Armenian version of Eusebius, the authority of Berosus is undisputed," I retain the unimportant assertion, simply because I have seen it disputed.

When he identifies Kedor Laomer, on Rawlinson's authority, with Kedor Mapula, I retain it as a sample of an unsatisfactory statement.

When he speaks of the Egyptian influence, still exerted over our medical practice, I strengthen his illustrations; and I could not refrain from adding, to his happy guess about the eras of migration, the confirmation furnished, since his death, by the discovery of the present practice of the Jews of Cochin China. It was furnished me by an eminent German Rabbi.

When I encounter variations of spelling, as an instance of which I may give the name of Raamses, spelled alternately as Ramses, Raamses, Rameses, Ramessis, and Remesis, I adhere to the mode which seems to show some phonetic value. I occasionally change a C to K, to show philological relations, although I may adhere to either letter throughout the body of the statement.

I am very well aware that Bunsen founded some unimportant theories on some mistaken valuation of the tablet literature of China. If the error should be great, that section of the subject will be worked up again in the light of Dr. Legge's revelations. The mistake casts no reproach upon the author. Those of us who recall the Latin translation of an arrow-headed inscription, once supposed to commemorate the neighing of the horse led by the groom of Darius, king of Persia, and remember how confidently it was relied upon, a few years since, by the most eminent philologists, have been amused, of late, by the new version, which dispels the fable, and proves the inscription to commemorate the natural productions of the district. Not on that account, however, do we distrust the scholars. When enthusiasm suggests an inference, honesty soon discovers the error. Bunsen's eyes were, for the most part, clear, and his purpose was wholly so.

Although I am aware that my own opinion, in reference to the matters treated in this book, is of small importance, I cannot send out this pamphlet without saying here, as I have said in private repeatedly, without eliciting any sympathy, that it seems to me purely chimerical for Bunsen to have based his chronological scheme on 21,000 years, rather than 25,000, or, more accurately, 25,791 years, the recognized period for the nutation of the ecliptic, for the revolution of the seasons, or the describing of a circle in the Heavens by the north pole of the earth.

What tempted him to pitch upon an arbitrary number of years, — which no one remembers, which no one will recognize, and which is, if I understand it, an imaginary period, being the time it *would* take for the revolution, if it were not for a certain delaying element in the axis of the earth itself, — I cannot imagine.

My common sense assures me that there is reason in this objection, though scientific people look as if I had suddenly gone mad, whenever I propose it. On this account, although it does not in the least disturb Bunsen's scheme, nor impair his conclusions, I had determined to say it boldly in print, when the first "crumb of comfort" was received from a most unexpected source.

As I sat here writing, there came to me, from Worcester, the "Proceedings of the Antiquarian Society," at its last annual meeting, Oct. 21, 1867. In the report of my friend, Mr. Haven, I find it suggested, that this very "revolution of the seasons" may account for "Icelandic literature and civilization, and for Pre-Columbian explorations of the Northern-American coast;" and, in connection with this, he prints the following note: —

"It is a scientific theory, that, by the conical movement of the polar axis of the earth, which causes the precession of the Equinoxes, the northern and southern hemispheres are subjected to influences increasing or diminishing their average temperature. When the northern half of the globe is growing warmer, the southern half will, in an equal proportion, be growing colder, and *vice versa*. The entire revolution has been calculated to require twenty-five thousand seven hundred and ninety-one years. It has been noticed, that, since the middle of the thirteenth century, the climate of all northern countries has gradually become colder, and the line of tropical vegetation has retreated towards the south, while the culture of the soil has been actually abandoned in latitudes where it was once practicable and productive. Thus, in the twelfth century, agriculture, commerce, and letters flourished in Iceland, which was the seat of a prosperous civilization. Communities of colonists existed in Greenland, having villages and churches and cultivated fields, like those of Norway and

Sweden; but they were cut off from all communication with the rest of the world, and probably destroyed, by the accumulation of ice, which has, for centuries, prevented approach to that side of the country. The glaciers of the Alps, it is well known, are extending. Roads, pastures, and even sites of habitation, formerly used and occupied, are now covered with perpetual snow. The advance of the glaciers, however, is not continuous, but dependent upon the character of the seasons. In very dry years, less snow is created, and the line of frost retreats: but, in each successive generation, the limit of vegetation is perceptibly lower.

"The inference is, that, in the northern hemisphere, another period of arctic temperature, over nearly its whole extent, is approaching, by slow but sure advances, and will culminate in about twelve thousand years, provided there is no interference, on the part of physical laws, whose nature and influence have not yet been ascertained."

It will be seen that Mr. Haven estimates this period as I do; and that, if *I* have lost *my* wits, *he* has lost *his* also. Do what I will, I cannot make 21,000 years represent, to my mind, a *real* period; but such is my respect for Bunsen, that I cannot refrain from the belief, that he perceived some adequate motive for its selection. What that motive was, it is not probable we shall ever know, unless he has left it recorded among unpublished memoranda.

Mr. Haven's notes contain one other matter of interest to the readers of this pamphlet.

I have stated that Dr. Birch found the evidences of highly advanced civilization, hidden in the Delta of the Nile, beneath the accretions of more than 11,000 years.

In the Delta, near Villeneuve, on the Lake of Geneva, Morlot assigns to the remains of the stone period a remoteness of 7,000 years.

Victor Gilliéron believes, from similar inferences, drawn,

however, from wholly independent premises, that the piles still standing at the Pont de Thielle, between Lakes Bienne and Neuchâtel, were driven 6,750 years ago!

In connection with what I have indicated of the labors of Hekekyan Bey, in the text, he tells us that Professor Carl Vogt, of Geneva, author of "The Natural History of Man," prefers the estimates of Hekekyan Bey to those of his Swiss cotemporaries. They accord very nearly, I believe, with those of Dr. Birch. In this report also, Mr. Haven tells us something of the work of Isaac La Peyrera, entitled "Præ-Adamitæ," published in Holland, in 1655, which was condemned to be burnt as a heresy. The author undertook to prove, *from the Scripture*, that the human race had existed for an indefinite period before Adam, — the words of Paul himself, that in "*Adam all died*," having started his mind upon this quest. He touches curiously enough much of Bunsen's ground, looks to the Esquimaux as the type of the Pre-Adamic races, and believes Adam to have been the ancestor of the Jews only, as Edom was the ancestor of the Phœnicians.

Mr. Haven introduces this man's name merely to allude to an English version of his book in the library of the Antiquarian Society.

Peyrera's reasonings are moderate; and he believes his own view, as Bunsen does, to be wholly consistent with reverent faith. It seems to me, therefore, that I cannot better conclude my Preface than by giving some account of this remarkable man, who believed little more than all the liberals of our day are expected to admit.

Isaac de la Peyrera was born at Bordeaux, of a noble family of Calvinists, in 1594. He was highly cultivated for his time, and accompanied Thuillerie on his Danish embassy. It was at Copenhagen that he entered on the course of *Septentrionale* studies, which resulted in a work on Iceland, another on Greenland, and finally in his Pre-Adamite *brochure*.

The last was published anonymously; and he was much surprised, while living tranquilly at Brussells, to find himself imprisoned by the order of the Archbishop of Malines. In prison, he lingered many months, and was finally freed through the influence of Condé, who procured his pardon from Alexander III., on condition of his embracing the Catholic faith. Poor Peyrera probably thought that there was little to choose between the intolerance of Calvinist and Catholic, and did as he was bid. Condé, it is asserted, had been shrewd enough to avoid all mention of a repudiation of Pre-Adamite ideas, which he continued to hold in full faith. He was the librarian of the Prince of Condé, and lived in Paris to the age of eighty-two. Here he published his accounts of Iceland and Greenland, including an account of the whale fishery, then unknown in Europe; also an account of the "Battle of Lens," fought by Condé; and "The Restoration of the Jews."

Then came in order the Pre-Adamite book in Latin, claiming that Moses' account of the origin of the Jewish nation in their ancestor, Adam, was one thing, and the account of the Creation, in the first chapter of Genesis, another, with a long, unrecorded history between. Bayle's Dictionary supplies the names of those who hastened to refute this terrible heresy.

He then published a "Letter," giving his reasons for his change of faith, and a series of letters addressed to the Comte de la Suze, to induce him to become a Catholic.

The lives of Peyrera and Bunsen furnish one of those

parallels which are always intensely interesting. The Homologon will be seen to be the more complete, when I state that the last work of Peyrera's life was a Latin commentary on the Bible, corresponding to Bunsen's "Bible Work." The "notes" of Peyrera were translated into French by the Abbé de Marolles. The impression was arrested by the order of the Church; but, in the "Bibliothèque du Roi," a few leaves may be found, which carry the reader through the twenty-third chapter of Leviticus. With the scanty resources of the sixteenth century,— before an arrow-headed inscription or hieroglyph had been interpreted, before a single expedition of investigation had been organized by Prussia, France, or England, before a lacustrine city was even dreamed of, — the clear and single eye of Peyrera penetrated to truths which seemed purely theoretical to his generation! There are few things in Europe I would travel so far to see as these broken leaves, which interpret his thoughts upon Genesis. His book reads tamely by the side of the sceptical rejections of more modern writers. Let his fate teach us to be generous to the exhaustive labors of Bunsen!

God never tires of creating his prophets, the exponents of protest, investigation, and pure devotion. Why should men tire, while striving to fulfil his purposes?

CAROLINE H. DALL.

141, WARREN AVENUE, BOSTON, U.S.A.
    March, 1868.

EGYPT'S PLACE IN HISTORY.

PART I.

A GENERAL SURVEY OF BUNSEN'S COMPETENCY, AND A SKETCH OF EGYPTIAN HISTORY.*

IN the long annals of mankind, there appears now and then a name which makes the whole world debtor. More commonly we find men who, by a certain brute force of will, turn the current of its life, and impress themselves, or at least their eccentricities and idiosyncracies, indelibly upon its succeeding waves. Of this latter class was John Calvin. Of the former was and is Christian Carl Josias Bunsen. With our hand upon his last volume, the English edition of which appears as the posthumous work of both author and translator, it seems to us that human immortality never found a nobler illustration. The work which survives testifies to the surviving soul. His five volumes suggest a design so magnificent; reveal a learning so wide, so varied, and so accurate; the plan of their publication suggests a faith in humanity so sincere, a faith in Truth, the author's God, so unwavering, — that the study of them is at once a satisfaction and an inspiration.

In history, Bunsen stands as Browning does in poetry, — self-possessed and erudite: having a passion for recondite

---

* Egypt's Place in Universal History. An Historical Investigation, in five books. By C. C. J. Baron Bunsen, D.Ph., D.C.L., and D.D. Translated from the German, by Charles H. Cottrell, Esq., M.A.; with Additions by Samuel Birch, LL.D. Vol. V. London: Longmans, Green, & Co., 1867.

learning, that few share; but so infatuated with his passion, that he perceives neither his own superiority nor the indifference of his rivals. His volumes need an editor who shall send an electric thread through their loose beads of argument, reconstruction, and perception; and, by drawing them within one coherent grasp, reveal alike the integrity of the pattern, and the simplicity with which it is wrought out. While waiting for this, we hope to draw attention to his studies, and put what is most valuable in them within the reach of those who can hardly expect to purchase one of the most expensive of modern books. It is the more important to do this, as a class of Egyptian scholars has now for the first time become possible.

When Bunsen began to work, Goodwin, Le Page Renouf, and Dr. Hincks were busy in England; Chabas, De Rougé, and Devéria, in France; Brugsch, Duemichen, Lauth, Lepsius, and Pleyte, in Germany; with a corps of assistants in each country, employed as translators or transcribers. No sooner did one of these men complete any section of his work, than it was published, or copied and sent to the others, that each might have the advantage of the labors of all. In especial, Lepsius and Bunsen exchanged papers, and published their great works in sections, that all possible light might be furnished by both at each advancing step. There was never a finer example of true communion in scholarship: each man fired with the zeal of knowledge, emulous only as to who should serve most; differing each from the other to the end, as to some important particulars, but never losing, through all, the sense of brotherhood and active trust; and each holding back the results of his own labor, till he had examined the work of the other.

Still greater obstacles to a popular knowledge of this book than the severe study it requires, may be found in the extent of acquisition demanded to make the reading of it profitable, and the great cost of the volumes themselves. Men may learn to study in time; they may grow in patience with a plan necessarily cumbersome; they may kindle into admiration, and acquire general learning, so as to fit themselves for appreciation: but there is no hope that the cost of these volumes will greatly diminish. That the Messrs. Longman should have been willing to furnish a font of hieroglyphic characters, at a cost such as is usually assumed only by foreign governments, seems somewhat like a miracle, and shows a generous zeal which this author was entitled to kindle.

No books ever published contain ampler learning of the sort that clergymen ought to acquire; none bear more directly, or with more telling force, on the modern debate as to the historic value of our Scriptures: yet they are books which it is hopeless to suppose that more than one clergyman in five hundred will ever glance over, much less study or possess.

In this country, we suppose, no man exists who is qualified to criticise them adequately. Is any qualified by knowledge of the great geologic convulsions which have prepared the globe for the habitation of man, he will fail, perhaps, in knowledge of the distribution of races, and of the philologic suggestions to be found in their own names, and those of their earliest localities. Should he fortunately be familiar with philologic ground, he may fail in intimate acquaintance with those remains of ancient literature which bear all the more truly, because indirectly, upon the great problems to be solved. Should he have mastered these, he must turn his attention to the sacred books and traditions of all Central Asiatic nations; our own Scripture must be set over against the Zend, the Vendidad, and the Vedas; and the absence of all tradition of a deluge in China and Egypt accounted for. Should he find himself competent to this problem, a severer one confronts him: he must arm himself with a special knowledge of the Semitic languages; and, when these have become familiar as his mother tongue, he must be prepared for a hieroglyphic or hieratic text, and not shrink from an investigation of the modern Coptic. Nor can he proceed without the widest general culture: for the history of Phœnicia must be ransacked for suggestive points; and rare mathematical and astronomical knowledge is required, that he may examine for himself all previous deductions as to the duration of cycles, the various means employed for the correction of the Julian year, and the possible origin of the various phases of Astral worship. Above all, he must be a man with his eyes wide open, who shall readily perceive the significance of all the small facts, daily coming into notice, upon the great problems to be solved. If we are to be governed by the estimate which Bunsen puts upon the labors of his English reviewers, in his fifth volume, England has produced no man better fitted for this work than the critics of our own country; but we need not be so governed, for, of the fairness of the few reviews that have appeared, common sense is a sufficiently competent judge.*

So far as Bunsen's reviewers have produced any effect upon the popular mind, it has probably been the creating of a certain distrust of Bunsen, founded upon the great difference between his estimate of the period required for the evolution of human civilization, and what is ordinarily called "Biblical chronology." It would be well if we could get rid of this Biblical chronology at the outset. Surely, very little scholarship is required to show, that the Bible actually of

* It is interesting to observe, that the same fond love of patient labor over minute details, which tends to make women eminent observers in astronomy, has already produced one Egyptologist, — Miss Corbaux. We find her, in 1855, writing an Introduction to a work on the so-called Exodus Papyri, by the Rev. J. D. Heath; and, although she started with a false theory, which vitiated her results, Baron Bunsen gives her candid praise, as the first English author who has entered upon the discussion of this subject, and as having intuitively seized, in her starting point, one of the most important problems to be solved.

itself makes no pretension to chronologic accuracy; and that the system which goes by its name, and has so long been active in manacling clergymen and oppressing scholars, is only a mass of Rabbinical corruptions, still further vitiated by the well-meant, but most dishonest, efforts of Eusebius and other early Christians, to force the whole records of the race into a certain conformity with a few numerical suggestions in the body of Holy Writ. Wherever Bunsen finds a numerical statement in the Scripture, however discrepant with actual facts, he expects to find an honest basis for the number, and looks for it.* It was as if by inspiration that he lighted in the beginning upon the period of " 21,000 years for the nutation of the ecliptic," as the proper field in which to work out his problem, — certainly not too large, when we consider that Dr. Birch has found the evidences of highly advanced civilization lying beneath the mud of the Delta, at a depth where the successive accretions of 11,000 years must have hidden them; and, if it is proper to judge of the age of long-buried lacustrine cities by the thickness of such over-deposits, why not admit the evidence when it relates to the manufacture of glass or the weaving of cloth? The 4,000 years of the Biblical chronology, Bunsen thinks an accurate measure of the beginning of national history on earth; or, what is equivalent, the beginning of our consciousness of continuous existence,

In the "Journal of Sacred Literature" for October, 1859, the author assumes a positive knowledge of early Egyptian history; the self-complacency of which shows him absolutely unable to appreciate the slow accumulative processes of Bunsen's investigations, and clinches the objections to his statements, regarding the residence in Egypt, with the child-

* A remarkable instance of this is to be found in the 215 years which the Jewish people were supposed to have passed in Egypt, — a numeration which he conclusively proves to refer to the period of their *oppression*, which they could not be supposed likely to forget, and beside which the pleasant memory of the long period of prosperous residence faded into thin air.

ish wonder, that, in the many attempts to reconstruct the extinct dynasties of Egypt, the statement in Isaiah, that "*the Assyrian* oppressed Israel without cause" should have been so *strangely neglected!* The passage (Isa. lii. 4), as it actually stands in the English version, gives some color to the reviewer's evident inference, that it was in Egypt that the Assyrian oppressed Israel: "For thus saith the Lord God, My people went down aforetime into Egypt, to sojourn there; and the Assyrian oppressed them without cause." * Surely there is no tolerable Hebrew scholar who will not admit, that, in the original, these two clauses have only this to do with each other, — that they are the separate stages of a climactic statement: once that unhappy people had been oppressed in Egypt; later, the Assyrian oppressed them without cause.†

The "Dublin Review" for February, 1860, if not as incompetent, is still more unfair. "In reference to the authenticity and credibility," it says, "of the remains now ascribed to Manetho, Baron Bunsen does not hesitate to say, that the numbers of Manetho have been transmitted to us quite as correctly as the canon of Ptolemy." Now, nothing is more evident, throughout the five volumes of Bunsen's work, than the constant effort of the author to correct the text of Manetho from Eratosthenes, the papyri, and the monuments. So far as we can judge, Manetho fell into hopeless chronological confusion, by attempting to give the sum of the *regnal* years in each dynasty, without regard to the orderly succession of reigns. For example, let us suppose that a prince of the house of Nantef should reign forty years, and then associate his son with him, surviving the association for thirty years. That the son, then reigning

*The whole difficulty lies in the punctuation, and the absence of a proper rhetorical inflection.
† Smith's Bible Dictionary, which echoes this criticism of the "Journal," manifests a personal hostility to Bunsen, which vitiates the conclusions in what should be some of the most valuable articles in that valuable book.

forty-two years, left his throne to a minor, a collateral heir, in charge of a regent who reigned twenty years. The heir might come to his throne at his majority, and reign thirty years, counting from the commencement of the regency but only ten in person. The actual period for which this house had been in possession of the throne, would be 40+42+20 +10; but Manetho would count 40+30+42+20+30, — the difference between 112 and 162, — indicating the exaggeration into which his method would lead him in three generations. This exaggeration is what Bunsen corrects, not out of his own imagination, but aided by the real State registers, deciphered since Lepsius.

A writer in the "Quarterly Review" for 1859 (p. 382 *et seq.*), remarks as follows: "Bunsen *assumes* that Manetho gave 3,555 years as the length of the Egyptian monarchy, and he then makes a mere conjecture the keystone of his arch." Now this may be a false deduction, not merely of Bunsen, but of Lepsius and Boekh; but it is not an assumption. It is a period wrought out by adherence to a theory based on acknowledged facts; assumed not by *one* man, but the then leading Egyptologists; and so little relied on by Bunsen as to be only once or twice adverted to. The reviewer goes on to object, that Manetho and Eratosthenes lived 3,000 years after the reigns their lists are supposed to authenticate; but what, in the mean time, has become of the contemporaneous lists on the monuments of the 3d and 4th dynasties, of the papyrus coeval with Moses, yet harmonizing with both Manetho and Eratosthenes? Does it become any critic of Bunsen to ignore the "Book of Kings," by Lepsius? So much, then, to show the manifest inadequacy of those who have endeavored to throw ridicule upon these magnificent labors, and to dissipate some bewildering mists. Fortunately for us, God provides against the natural incredulity of man. It is never left to any one person to stem the tide of historical unbelief. Converging lines of investigation, converging results of varied conscientious labors, sooner or later, burn all vital and necessary convictions into human consciousness.

At a recent meeting of the Palestinian Exploration Society, at Oxford, which met, we believe, to examine the photographs of the synagogue recently reconstructed at Capernaum, — the only building now to be identified in which it is known that Jesus of Nazareth once stood; a building reconstructed, it is said, after all these years, without the loss of a single stone, — Sir Henry Rawlinson said, that the excavations now going on at Jerusalem would give us a more exact knowledge of a long period of Hebrew history, than we possess of any similar period in the Greek and Roman; but an assertion like this, some time before, from Bunsen, met with no reception but ridicule. When, a little before his death, a new translation of a long-coveted papyrus was brought him, his attendant lamented that it would not be in his power to devote much attention to it; but a joyful light beamed in the eyes of the prostrate scholar, and, as his dying hand added a few notes to the manuscript, he murmured audibly, "It will come so soon, it will come so soon, — the justification of more than I ever dreamed!" Very lately, the French Minister of Public Instruction received a letter from M. Lejean, sent by the French Government to explore the Persian Gulf and its immediate vicinity. He believes himself to have discovered ante-Sanscrit idioms, — to use his own language, *langues paléoariennes*, — still spoken, in a district lying between Kashmir and Afghanistan, by certain mountain tribes; and he thinks these languages more allied to the European tongues than to the Sanscrit itself. In the Persian Gulf, he has followed, step by step, the course of Nearchus, who commanded the fleet of Alexander, and of whose voyage some account is preserved in Arrian. He has also traced the ruins of two Persepolitan cities, whose names have been preserved, the Messambria and Hierametis of Nearchus. At the same time, Unger, the Viennese palæontologist, writes from the pyramid of Dashoor, that in the unburnt bricks of which it is built, bricks moulded and laid at least as early as 3400 B.C., he has discovered manufactured substances, giving evidence of the high civilization already claimed for that period. Recent excavations of Yemenite ruins show, through the Himyarite inscriptions in the cities of Southern Arabia, that a race speaking and writing the same language dwelt in ancient Abyssinia, and on the shores across the straits; the certainty of a hitherto conjectured identity of races throwing much light on many points of Biblical criticism. Rawlinson tells us that the ancient Egyptians thoroughly understood the motive power of steam. The remains of fine Egyptian pottery in the oldest Etruscan tombs; the more recent finding of glass bottles, with Chinese inscriptions upon them, in the oldest tombs at Thebes, — suggest not only the immense antiquity of an almost universal commerce, but show how little effect the most valuable discovery, even that of the art of printing, can have upon a yet undeveloped people. First discoveries, like the discovery of sulphuric ether as an anæsthetic agent, seem merely tentative. This last discovery was useless, until a certain amount of general surgical skill made its practical employment necessary on the one hand, and safe on the other. So the art of printing has availed little in China, — so little, that its use never penetrated to the nations brought into the closest contact with that people. The cities of Bashan are at last uncovered; and the enormous rollers of stone, on which King Og threw back his portal, are now revealed to modern eyes. On the other hand, the intelligent zeal of Mr. Wilkinson, the English consul at Saloniki, has proved the authentic use of the word "politarch," in the eighth verse of the seventeenth chapter of Acts. The use of this word, in relation to a city not known to have any such officer, has been used as an argument against the age of the original manuscript. The exhuming of a buried arch, bearing an inscription in honor of events which took place under the administration of certain "politarchs," has put that question to rest. While critics debate the possible authorship and antiquity of the books of Moses, we are forced to acknowledge the age and authenticity of the Turin papyrus, sealed into a sarcophagus nineteen centuries before Christ, and the anonymous, ritualistic "Book of the Dead," written at least four thousand five hundred years ago; and, in more direct support of Baron Bunsen's work, we have a treatise recently published by the astronomer of the King of Egypt, Mahmoud Bey. The late viceroy, Said Pacha, ordered from him an astronomical investigation into the relation of the structure of the Pyramids to the dates of their erection. It was obvious that the great pyramid at Ghizeh was built when the rays of Sirius, in passing the meridian of Ghizeh, fell vertically on the south side. A prolonged calculation shows that this happened 3300 years B.C. The bearing of this calculation is seen, when we state that Bunsen had already fixed the year 3329 as that of the beginning of the reign of Cheops, by whom this pyramid was built.

But, before giving an account of Bunsen's work, we will speak briefly of the man himself.

Christian Carl Josias Bunsen, chevalier, statesman, philosopher, and theologian, was born, Aug. 25, 1791, at Corbach, the capital of the principality of Waldeck. He studied first at Marburg, and then under the celebrated Heyne at Göttingen. To his own natural bias was now added the impetus given by the influence of the greatest philologist of the time, — an enthusiastic archæologist, and a man whose reputation for integrity had already passed into a proverb. It was quite in keeping with the fact, that his first profound studies were pursued under the master who had done so much to revive a knowledge of Greek and Roman antiquities, that he first came to distinction by winning an academical prize, at the age of twenty-two, for a disquisition on "Athenian Laws of Descent." He then went to Holland and Denmark, to pursue at his leisure a careful study of the tongues spoken in Iceland, Scandinavia, and Friesland. In 1815, he began to study with Niebuhr, whose character and pursuits were still further adapted to educate him for the work he was to undertake. In 1816, he went to Paris, to study the Eastern tongues under Sylvestre de Sacy, then the first living Orientalist. In addition to holding the Persian professorship in the College de France, De Sacy was at this time rector of the University of Paris; and he was a literary man of such value and distinction, that, finding it impossible to replace him, Napoleon had been obliged to retain him in office after he had refused to take the oath of hatred to royalty. His Arabic grammar and anthology are still in use; and, as a Persian scholar, he has never been surpassed. While Bunsen was at Paris, Niebuhr had gone as Prussian minister to Rome; and, as soon as he quitted De Sacy, he joined his former teacher as secretary of legation. He met at Rome the King of Prussia, whom he greatly interested by his marked Protestant ardor; and, in 1824, several important changes were wrought in the relations of the Prussian Church and State by his influence over the king. In 1827, he succeeded Niebuhr as Prussian Minister; but, not being able to influence the Papal See to the extent of his desires, he resigned his position in 1837, or rather exchanged it for that of Minister to the Swiss Federation. In 1841, he was appointed Minister to England, to consult the English Government on the formation of a Protestant bishopric, which he fondly hoped would secure the interests of reform; and he was, later, more formally appointed Minister to the Court of St. James. At that time he wrote in German, and printed, we believe at

Hamburg, his work on "The Constitution of the Church of the Future," afterwards translated and printed at London in 1847. It is probable that the political prejudice excited against this Prussian project, which all parties seem to have shared, created an impression unfavorable to the reception of his more scholarly work. Bunsen believed in the possibility of a Christian nation, — of a Christian state. The manner in which this Church was linked to cumbrous Prussian machinery made it seem to most men impracticable and absurd, a fair mark for ridicule, and gave to his own name and Gladstone's an unenviable prominence for the time. Niebuhr had studied at Edinburgh; and, while with him in Rome, Bunsen had married the daughter of an English clergyman. From that time, England seems to have divided his affections with his native country, and some of his most valuable studies were pursued at the British Museum. At the request of his king, he presented to the Court of Prussia a memorial upon the formation of a constitutional government like that of England. He favored the cause of Schleswig-Holstein, and, by a memoir to Palmerston, protested against England's attitude in regard to it. Sympathizing with the Western allies, rather than with Prussia, he resigned his position, at the beginning of the Eastern war in 1853, and removed to Heidelberg, where he was at once regarded as the leader in all matters relating to Christian liberty.

His most distinguished works, beside that under review, are "Hippolytus and his Times" (two volumes, Leipsic, 1853), and "Complete Bible-work for the Christian Community" (two volumes, Brockhaus, Leipsic, 1853). The latter work is divided into three parts, — the first giving the newly translated text of the Old and New Testament, with abundant notes; the second is the completion of the first, containing Bible texts historically arranged and explained; and the third consists of treatises on various subjects, such as the "Everlasting Kingdom" and the "Life of Jesus." This book had not attained its perfect form at the time of his death.

"Egypt's Place in History" was published at Hamburg and Göttingen in five volumes, from 1845 to 1860; and the English translation followed rapidly upon the German issue. The last volume, however, has only just come to this country, having been published about the last of May. Its contents, which are at this moment of special interest to the scholar, may be briefly noted here. It contains, first, a final statement of the Problems to be solved; then the Key to these problems. In this Key we have, 1st, A solution of Problems exclusively Egyptian, under which the first and second problems of the third dynasty, and the problem of the builders of the Great Pyramids, are treated; 2d, Chronological results connected with Biblical, Assyrian, Babylonian, and Greek synchronisms, giving points of contact before and after Solomon; 3d, Results connected with the Problem of reconstructing the ancient ante-chronological, but epochal, history of Egypt; 4th, Corollaries, philosophical and practical. In this final treatment, Bunsen draws in the slides of his telescope, and rests upon the acknowledged Alexandrian chronology in reference to Egypt, — a chronology, however, which does not bring the construction of the Great Pyramid so nearly into the place assigned it by Mahmoud Bey, as his own theoretic extension. Then follows an Appendix, in which the Baron examines the position of his reviewers; and then — that which gives to this work its special value, and puts it in the power of every scholar to become a critic, if he will — Dr. Birch's translation of the "Book of the Dead;" a Dictionary of Hieroglyphics occupying 150 pages; a Hieroglyphic Grammar occupying 130 pages; and thirteen selected Egyptian texts, with their translations, — these texts being among the most valuable for purposes of Bibilical criticism. This is followed by fifty pages devoted to a comparison of old and new Egyptian words, and to a comparison of these with the Semitic and Iranian; and, finally, we have the fragments of Philo Byblus, with comments by Dr. Bernays, and a revision and Latin preface by Bunsen, completed, we believe, only a short time before his death.

That this pupil of Heyne, Niebuhr, and Champollion (with whom Bunsen studied at Rome in 1826) should be only half prepared for his great work, was manifestly impossible. The story we have told shows that he was fitted for it, not only by his philological and archæological studies, not only by a rare knowledge of language, science, history, and governments, but by personal contact, prolonged and close, with the most eminent scholars of his day in the same walks, by an ardent devotion to Protestant Christianity, his love of Christian liberty, and his freedom from all fear that any efforts of his could shake the foundations of eternal truth. As a politician, he was from the beginning fastidiously conscientious. There is, indeed, one reason why those who know Bunsen well will hardly expect his labors to come to speedy appreciation. He was, as a man, far too well balanced to challenge immediate sympathy; he held out his hand cordially to both the left wing and the right; he could see truth and zeal on the side of his opponents. And while, on the one hand, he fearlessly laid Theology under his scalpel, on the other, he treated its dead body with reverent consideration. *Fanaticism is far more acceptable to mankind than a radical toleration.*

Of the last months of his life we have no trustworthy account, although it is quite possible that such an account is in existence. His beautiful last words, spoken to the beloved English wife who leaned over his pillow, have floated across the Atlantic, and touched all our hearts: "In thy face have I seen the Eternal."

We have now to consider the way in which Bunsen approaches the great historical problem he has attempted to solve. First, then, in reference to the period that he selects in which to evolve and develop the history of races. He was too shrewd a man not to see, that the greatest difficulty in the reconstruction of ancient history had always lain in the want of room in which to deploy the grand army of facts,—especially for the growth of language, according to the known conditions of its development. He wished, therefore, for a natural period, of a length which was sufficient to allow for the development of the earliest civilizations. As nothing seems to ordinary readers more chimerical than his selection, we wish to add a popular statement to the commonly incomprehensible figures of the scientist. It is well known to most people, that there is a marked change in the apparent position of the constellations since that was first recorded by the ancients. To say nothing of the ante-historic periods, other pole-stars than ours have been in use at various times in the world's history. The axis of the earth does not point steadily to the tail of the Little Bear, but the North Pole itself describes a circle in the heavens. It moves towards the West; therefore the constellations travel farther and farther to the East, which was early discovered by Chinese astronomers, and, before the time of Christ, by Hipparchus of Rhodes. The common phrase, "precession of the equinoxes," is the strict way of expressing this fact. The change in the position of the axis is occasioned by the irregular attraction of both sun and moon. The greatest irregularity is produced by the moon; but, owing to her own changes of position, she cannot produce it with steadiness, and therefore our axis describes its circle in the heavens in a tremulous way,—moving a little forward, and then a little back, and so on. There is no more delicate work for the astronomer than to consider all these forces, note their variations, and arrive at a correct result. Newton did not succeed in doing it. D'Alembert and La Place did; and, since the time of the latter, it is customary to say, that the axis of the earth describes its complete circle in the heavens in the space of 25,000 years; reduced, by the revolution of the apsides, to the 21,000, which Bunsen calls the "nutation of the ecliptic."

Now, it is obvious to every one, that any considerable change in the position of the axis of the earth would create a change in the climate of the various zones; and, as the development of the races of mankind has a great deal to do with climate, it was natural that a period which affords such changes should attract the man of science. But the 21,000 years allowed for this nutation of the ecliptic, presents to the Northern Hemisphere, in which mankind have developed, two points, — one *unfavorable*, in which the winter gains eight days of cold; one *favorable*, in which summer gains eight days of heat: and the cycle is supposed to have closed with the favorable period in the year 1248 of our era, the favorable circumstances attending to a degree, many years, both before and after that date. The unfavorable point would be 10,000 years B.C., with a like attendance of unfavorable circumstances. Now, the work of creation would necessarily demand the finest influences; and the great geologic changes, which are indicated by the flood, would be most likely to occur at the period of climatic depression. We take the period of 10,000 years B.C., as the proper period for the flood, and we go back 21,000 years from the favorable point of one thousand two hundred and forty-eight in our era, to another corresponding to it, — 20,000 years B.C., — for the period of man's creation, which took place in the greatest possible fulness of light and life.

He takes, as the basis of his chronological scheme, therefore, the astronomical cycle of 21,000 years, — the period during which our summer solstice falls successively in every portion of the earth's orbit.* At present, as is well known, the summer in the northern hemisphere is at the time of the earth's greatest distance from the sun; hence the season is longer and more temperate: while, in the southern hemisphere, the summer is hotter and fiercer, the winter longer and colder, than in the same latitude at the north. Our summer season, reckoning from the vernal to the autumnal equinox, is thus eight days longer than our winter; and this may be called, for us, the favorable portion of the cycle. The most favorable moment occurs when the solstitial point — that is, the sun's highest northern declination — falls exactly at the portion of the orbit farthest from the sun: this moment (which we may call the noon of the favorable period) fell, by the reckoning of astronomers, in the year A.D. 1248.

But Bunsen supposes that a greater climatic change was wrought at the period known as that of the Flood, than would have occurred in the natural order of things. The slightest preponderance of matter at any point of the earth's surface will necessarily alter the relations of the poles to the plane of the ecliptic. Should this occur suddenly, by any monstrous volcanic action, such as would uplift a continent, the change in the inclination of the axis would be very sudden, and might alter all the conditions of terrene

---

* This period is obtained as follows: Adding together 50.1" (the annual amount of the retreat of the equinoctial point in the heavens, owing to the phenomenon called "precession of the equinoxes") to 11.8" (the annual amount of the "revolution of the apsides," in the contrary direction), we obtain 61.9" for the annual motion of the point of the earth's aphelion relative to the nodes of the ecliptic; and, dividing by this the whole number of seconds in 360 degrees (1,296,000), we find the above number, 21,000 (more precisely, 20,985), for the cycle of the revolution of the seasons.

In virtue of "precession," modified by "nutation," the terrestrial pole describes a tremulous circle in the heavens, of about 47° diameter, about the pole of the ecliptic, once in 25,868 years. The several stars which are thus made successively "pole-stars" to the earth, afford an important element in fixing some of the cardinal dates in Egyptian history.

life. If Greenland were to be loosed from the bottom of the sea, and were to float into the southern hemisphere, the whole climate of the globe would change; nay, it is hardly too violent a supposition to say that the tropics and the poles might possibly change places. We have such evidences of convulsion stamped into the geologic history of the earth, — traces of tropical vegetation and mammoth existences so near the poles; traces of marine botany and ocean life on Alpine heights, — that it would seem as if such changes must have taken place, whether before or after the creation of man; and, if so, the present inclination of the earth's axis may be a comparatively modern thing. The longest diameter of a planet must sway it to the sun; and, when the substance is heaped up so as to bring this length into a new place, there will be an entire change of climate, genera, and species. Old coasts would sink, reefs rise, and seas disappear or be created. There seem to be indications of such changes in the positions of still other planets. This explanation, nowhere offered in detail by our author, we are obliged to assume for him, or leave his conclusions as to the pre-delugic period in such uncertainty as must greatly detract from their usefulness.

But this only gives to Baron Bunsen the blank paper on which he is to draw his chart. Let us see what it is that he really has to do, and whether the task should be impossible. Let us suppose that the inhabitants of North America, driven, by a submerging storm of sand and rain, from their own shore, with the traces of their civilization and every fragment of native literature destroyed, should seek a refuge in South America, and ultimately desire a map of the land, as it was before its terrible overflow. Behring's Straits, the Isthmus of Darien, the projecting peninsula of Florida, still suggest some boundaries. There is a tradition of the great lakes and Niagara, of the Alleghanies and the Rocky Mountains, and of the fertile bottom lying between, drained by an enormous river, unlike any on the globe. An adventurous geologist visits the deserted land, finds the Rocky Mountains in their place, but has so little idea of the proper scale of things, that he does not go far enough off for the traces of Niagara and Plymouth Rock. He comes home, and rants about the delusion of those who believe in such places. There is no chain of lakes. As he descended from the heights, did he not touch the very sea-coast, at a place still inhabited by a degraded race, and called by an old name, Matagorda? They, too, had some old traditions about Washington, and Plymouth Rock; but who would believe them? Meanwhile, the literary people have been busy. With no books of their own past to fall back upon, they have ransacked all Europe for fragments of old literature relating to the extinct nation. One copy of old Botta had been exhumed from the dust of libraries, and seems to give some color to the traditions they themselves believe; but, just as they are delighting themselves with the grim old chronicle, a multitude of copies of a certain book are found beneath the fallen ruins of a portion of the British Museum. It is evidently a school-book, printed, for the instruction of children, nearly half a century later than old Botta, in 1859, at London, Eng.; and it consists of questions and answers, some of them running thus: *Q*. What countries lie to the south of the great lakes? *A*. Two: the United States and Washington. *Q*. What people inhabit these countries? *A*. White people, Indians, and the more civilized Mexicans. The literary people send in haste for the geologist. They hope, like Professor Cleveland, that they are "descended from the more civilized Mexicans;"* but the geologist looks at the philologist, and smiles. "Mexicans!" said he, "that is what the

---

* The school-book alluded to formed the subject of a humorous address by Professor Cleveland, at a consular dinner given to him, at Cardiff, in Wales.

people call themselves, whom I found at Matagorda: they never heard of the great lakes. You may depend upon it, old Botta was writing an historical romance, — stupid work he made of it, to be sure." But there is one of the literary guild, a little more depressed than the rest: he holds up a book, once dressed in gayest colors. It is called "New America." "According to this," he says, "our ancestors were bold marauders. Somewhere near your Rocky Mountains, they had a grand harem, and preached the Gospel of Polygamy. Farther to the east, a tribe of Amazons lived; they denied the possession of any high gifts to the male sex, but were themselves prophets, priests, and seers, whose sight reached back to an antediluvian period." "Polygamy!" said the geologist, rubbing his forehead. "On the plains at the foot of the Rocky Mountains, I came upon an enormous mount. It represented a serpent wound round the Cosmic egg, with his tail in his mouth. I thought then that it was accidental; but we must send off a party to explore. What, after all, if we could trace these people to the polygamists of Eastern Asia?"—"No," interrupts a younger student. "I am sure I find traces in some of their fragments of an Egyptian connection. A certain sect must have worshipped the great eye of the world,—in short, Osiris!"

Now, in just such a position as this were the Egyptologists, when Champollion deciphered the Rosetta stone; and the deciphering of the Tablets of Karnak and Abydos, and the Royal Papyrus, have produced upon this confusion precisely the same effect that the exhuming of all the Records of the State Department at Washington, with their attendant documents, would produce upon our supposed friends in South America.

Before coming to the historical results Bunsen considers himself to have attained, it is necessary to explain still another point, — the history of the Egyptian year. If any man of the present day wishes to prove himself descended from some remote, distinguished ancestor, he in the first instance traces the family of that ancestor as far down as possible, and then carries his own as far up as possible. If at the point of junction, where the keystone of his arch of evidence should be, he finds only a void, he must search on one side for that which may give indirect evidence of its previous existence. The fallen stone is often found far from its original bed. Now, in the genealogy of the world, the history of Egypt is this keystone. It is a bridge connecting modern life with ancient; and its well-kept registers, to which even Herodotus refers, abound in synchronisms, which assist us to reconstruct other histories as well. It would seem as if its golden sands, its dry atmosphere, and its perished civilization, had been permitted by Providence, in order that the secret of the world's life should be preserved, and no foot of progress stamp out the traces of the world's early and uncertain march. The papyri, tablets, and sarcophagi of Egypt begin to decay when they are placed in Northern museums. We hope the time will come when scholars will press the erection of a museum on her own soil, which shall preserve, and not destroy, and of which all the powers of the civilized world shall become the guardians. The removal of colored bas-reliefs and frescoes has already proved conclusively, that the secret of their long preservation lies in climate, and not in the skill of ancient art.

The Egyptians divided the year into three seasons; viz., —

1. The Green Season;
2. The Harvest;
3. The Inundation;

— each consisting of four months of thirty days. Now, the beginning of one of these seasons, at the era when this division of time first occurred, is fixed for us by one of the great natural facts of the country. The first day of the inundation invariably coincides, at Syene, with the summer solstice. Just at that period the waters of the Nile begin to overflow. The ordinary Egyptian year consisted of twelve months of thirty days each, with only five days added at the close. So, failing to count in the six hours of surplus time remaining at the close of each year, every four years a day was lost, and the season of the inundation was noted one day too soon. In 365 times four, or 1,460 years, it would be noted a whole year too soon; and a whole year must be thrown in to correct the error and equalize solar and lunar notation. Therefore, every fourteen hundred and sixty-first completed a cycle by a sacred, festive year.

The Egyptians had, besides, a civil year; and we trust that patient attention will be given to our attempt to explain this in a simple way. The restoration of all the ancient chronology of Egypt depends upon the place of this festive year, which was observed as sacred to a very late period of Egyptian history; and, from the later and certainly historic celebrations of it, we must ascend to the period of its institution. Now, this kind of notation was in use in the time of Menes, the first recorded king; that is, as early as 3400 B.C. Let us assume, therefore, that, at the next previous point in time, when the first day of the first month of the season of inundation fell on the solstice, was the period of institution. It may have been 1,460 years earlier; but it must have been as old as that. Here is the order of the seasons, each consisting of four months:—

First Tetrameny, or Green Season.

1. Thoth (opener of the year . . . . November.
2. Paophi . . . . December.
3. Hathor . . . . January.
4. Choriack. . . . . February.

Second Tetrameny, or Harvest Season.

5. Toby . . . . March.
6. Mechir . . . . April.
7. Phamenoth . . . . May.
8. Pharmuthi . . . . June.

Third Tetrameny, or the Inundation.

9. Pachon . . . . July.
10. Paôni . . . . August.
11. Epiphi (Hebrew, *Ebib*, or *Abib*) . . September.
12. Mesori . . . . October.*

Now it is evident, that, when this system first came into use, the summer solstice fell on the 1st of Pachon, and the winter equinox on the 1st of Mesori. The Hebrews carried out of Egypt the name of the eleventh month, *Epiphi*, on the 14th of which they crossed the Red Sea. In the twelfth chapter of Exodus, it is written that they were at this time commanded to alter their calendar, and to begin the year with the month Ebib. We wish any words of ours could direct the attention of Egyptologists towards one important inference, hitherto neglected. It is about as well established as any point can be, that the year of Exodus falls between 1314 B.C. and 1320 B.C. Hillel, we believe, ascribes it to the year 1314. Now, it is certain, that, if we can find the year, within this limit, in which the 14th of Epiphi fell on the first full moon of the spring, — about the 14th of our April, at which date the Passover has always been celebrated, — we shall find the exact date of the Exodus. On the other hand, it would seem as if the modern Jewish practice, of beginning the year at the autumnal equinox, had some faint and hidden reference to the original

---

* It is obvious that the English names attached to these months are not strictly accurate, — only approximate. For example, the first day of the period of the inundation, or the month Pachon, did not properly fall on the 1st of July, but on the solstitial point, the 22d of June.

place of Epiphi in the Egyptian calendar, or was adjusted to it by Hillel.

Censorinus tells us, that the Egyptians had a great Sothiac year. It began whenever the sun rose at the same moment as the Dog Star. This could happen only once in 1,460 years, when the solar and lunar years met and were made one. One such sacred year was recorded 1,322 years before Christ. Cycles began, therefore, in the years —

4242 B.C.
2782 B.C.
1322 B.C.

Now, we have seen that Thoth was the first month of the Egyptian year; and its proper place was unchangeably fixed at 120 days after the solstice. It fell in the right place in the years—

3285 B.C.
1780 B.C.

Of these five eras, 3285 * B.C. must have been the most remarkable; for then the sun rose with Sirius at the solstice (or seemed so to rise), and the 1st of Thoth fell on the required moment.† About this time, then, Bunsen supposes this calendar to have been instituted. We can see how they came, in time, to have two calendars. The civil year must begin with the first of Thoth, no matter how far it had slipped back from its place. The sacred Sothiac year must always begin at the rising of Sirius. They intercalated nothing, but noted the periodical loss, so as to interpolate one year into the calendar once in every 1,460 years. In one Sothiac cycle, the beginning of the year moved through

---

* Bunsen does not explain; but it would seem as if these two dates must have been conformed to the Phœnix cycle, and not to the Sothiac.

† If we accept the astronomical conclusions of Mahmoud Bey, is it not quite probable that the Great Pyramid of Ghizeh was begun this year, to mark and commemorate these extraordinary coincidences?

every part of the heavens; which may possibly explain the mystical saying of the priests, when they told Herodotus, that, between the reigns of Menes and Sethos, *the sun had twice risen in the west.* That is, this movable solar year had twice begun at the indicated place in the heavens.

It was only another way of concealing the sacred year, when it was said that the phœnix rose from its ashes once in 1,500 years. This name, so long believed to be that of a fabulous bird, is, in the original, equivalent to *sæculum*, or "period of years." Its story conveyed the error of the Julian year. The three periods of the Solar or Phœnix cycle had a sort of correspondence to the three divisions of the common year. The first day of the new year was placed unchangeably, as we have said, 120 days after the solstice; and, when the rising of Sirius corresponded to this solstice, the grand cycle would begin with the succeeding new year. The secret was kept, but the key was preserved. We can find it in the story Plutarch tells of Hermes. Hermes played at dice with Selene (the moon), and won from her five days. Chronos and Netpé (the starry Time and the starry Space), having been privately married, begat five children, — the five Planets. The Sun discovered it, and was enraged; for there was neither Space nor Time for new stars. He cursed Netpé, therefore, saying that her children should be born neither into month nor year. Netpé, in her distress, appealed to Thoth, god of wisdom and of stars. He, having embraced her, played again with the moon, and won from her the seventy-second part of every day in the year of 360 days. Out of these he formed five days, which he threw in at the end of twelve months. In these days, the waiting planets were born; and not only they, but the five gods who live in them, came into the world. Osiris, Typhon, Horus, Isis, and Nepthys came into the world on these days: so the sacred year was made up of the birthdays of the gods, — truly a "divine year"! *

We have given to Baron Bunsen the blank paper on which he is to draw his chart; namely, the 21,000 years. We will sketch the finished map lightly, according to the natural order of events, rather than to the order of investigation. Before we enter upon this work, one or two things must be fixed in the mind. The first historic king of Egypt is supposed to have reigned about 3,400 years before Christ; but he united under himself twenty-seven different provinces, of a civilization already far advanced. He found, when he ascended the throne, a perfect language, and a ceremonial religion fully developed. His name was Menes, and he stands as the representative of the beginning of history to Egypt. After his time, its history is divided into three parts: —

1. The Old Empire, ot the empire of Menes, lasting 1,076 years, and ending with the thirteenth dynasty.

2. The Middle Empire, of Hyksos or shepherd kings, mixed with subordinate native princes, lasting 922 years, and ending with the seventeenth dynasty.

3. The New Empire, a revival of native Egyptian power, which expelled the Hyksos, lasting 1,286 years, and ending with the thirtieth dynasty.†

It will thus be seen, that the history of Egypt contains the history of thirty different dynasties, or reigning families, — not necessarily Egyptian, only *reigning* in Egypt.

* This Phœnix cycle, consisting of three periods of 500 years each, must have been founded on the Apis year, — equal to twenty times 360 days; that is, 500 years. This notation was probably an older method than the Sothiac of reaching the same result; and was recognized by the grand multiple of the Apis and Sothiac cycles, which was supposed to produce a grand cosmic year.

† Written lists of Manetho and Eratosthenes, statements of Herodotus, Diodorus, Apollodorus, and others, two monumental tablets, and several valuable papyrus lists of kings, furnish evidence in relation to these periods, beside that found in pyramids and tombs.

Thus, the twenty-eighth dynasty consisted of Cambyses, Darius, and Xerxes, better known in connection with Persia. At first, historians were determined that these dynasties should indicate families reigning in succession: but the truth is, that many of these princes were reigning together; that the royal power of one or another was frequently maintained only in some remote province; and, as to the numbers of the dynasties, they were given arbitrarily, and are no guide whatever to the order of succession. Thus, for example, the seventh, eighth, ninth, tenth, and eleventh were all on the throne together; the ninth and tenth being a continuation of the fifth at Heracleapolis, the seventh and eighth reigning at Memphis, and the eleventh at Thebes.

We next proceed to give Bunsen's historical and astronomical checks for the age of the human race.

1. Mankind was created, geographically, on the northern slope of the Hindu Kush, and its continuation to the Taurus and the open Polar Sea, in which the Ural was then an island or a peninsula; the northern part of Europe and Asia not being as yet in existence. The eastern limit was formed by the Chinese Altai; the western, by Ararat and the Caspian Caucasus. From the east flowed the rivers called Oxus and Jaxartes; from the west, the Tigris and Euphrates, — the four rivers of which there is an almost universal tradition.

2. A vast catastrophe by fire and water, which formed the Aral and Caspian Seas, involving a great change of climate, drove them down from this slope. What had been a delicious country, now became cold and unproductive, or arid from burning heat. That this convulsion created a great change in the distribution of races, the Bible and the Vendidad (one of the books of the Zend) show. In that primeval world there was already high antiquity and a good deal of civilization. Now, we have already explained the period we have allowed for the development of mankind previous to

the Deluge. We have stated that in 1248 A.D. our summer gained eight days, and the whole climate of the northern hemisphere was in a favorable condition. In A.D. 6498, the two seasons will be in equilibrium; and in 11,748 the cold season will have gained eight days. If we calculate backward, we shall find that at B.C. 4002 the seasons were in equilibrium; that at B.C. 9252 cold weather and unfavorable conditions reigned; and that the maximum of heat had been reached 19,752 B.C. For this reason, the creation of man has been assigned to the twentieth century before the Christian era; and the Flood, with its attendant catastrophes, to the tenth.

Here we insert a table of conclusions, which seem needed to carry on the story. Before the Deluge, our Scripture tells us, Cain emigrated from Eden. He went toward the East, and became the father of Turanian civilization. Neither the carefully kept books of the Chinese nor the Egyptian records show any knowledge of the Flood: consequently, the races who founded these two civilizations emigrated from the primal land before the Flood. The Hindoos have long been considered a very ancient race; but this opinion is a mistake: a feud divided them from the main body of the Iranians, commonly called Persians, as late as 6000 B.C. The Zend contains only a record of primeval migrations, founding fourteen kingdoms, — the last in the Punjaub. The ancestral Aryans left Iran proper, "the land of pleasantness," on account of a great convulsion of nature near the sources of the Oxus and Jaxartes. This was on the slopes of Belur Tagh, between 40° and 37° north latitude, and 89° or 90° east longitude. Two months of summer to ten of winter describes the climate which they left. The Zend traces the original catastrophe to water, ice, and upheaval; a part of our Scripture traces it to water only: but we must not forget the flames which guarded the gates of Eden, in the still older story.

The original seat of Zoroaster was in Bactria, where he ruled after the time of Menes. In the Gâthâs of Jasma his Zend was called the Maga; but there was a great difference between his trinity of "thought, word, and deed," and the corrupted Magism. From the Zend we get a table like this:—

	B.C.
Plutonic disturbance and primeval emigration	10,000
Gradual separation into Germans, Sclaves, &c.	8,000
Gradual extension of races, on to	5,000
Aryan emigration to the Punjaub	4,000
Zoroaster's religious reform	3,500
Sanscrit ceasing to be a living language	1,000

The two great formative branches of the human family show indelible marks of their common origin. The Semitic and Aryan commenced an independent progression at the very moment when Egypt became stationary.

In Babylon the two branches met. There was no root in Hebrew or Chaldean, for the Maga, or the Mighty. It was the result of Aryan thought working through the Chaldean. Abraham escaped from it by migration. There are no common indications between his dialect and the language of the Zend.

From the Vendidad we take the following abbreviated record of their movements:—

1. They went north, to Samarcand, driven by a raging pestilence;

2. To Margiana, where they encountered wars and invading Cossacks;

3. To Bactria, where they found mosquitoes and poisonous plants;

4. To Nisaya, in Northern Parthia, where religious scepticism assailed them;

5. To Herat, where they encountered toil and poverty;

6. To Segestan-Dushak, where schism again assailed them;

7. To Caboul;

8. To Candahar, invaded by the terrible sin of pæderasty, or unnatural lust;

9. To Haraquaiti, where an apostacy, concerning the burial of the dead, occurred;

10. To Hetumat, the classic Etymander, where sorcery prevailed;

11. To Northern Media, where schism began again;

12. To Khorassan, where the profane burning of the dead was introduced;

13. To Verena, or Ghilan, where illness assailed their women;

14. To the Punjaub, where they finally separated into Persians and Hindus;

In Irania, *Ary* meant Lord; in Egypt, it kept the same signification.

The condition of mankind, before this separation, was stereotyped on the Nile. It will be remembered, that the Egyptians were the descendants of Kham or Chem, or, more popularly, Ham. We shall confine ourselves, as far as possible, to the use of the first term.

From this train of thought, and much evidence, which we must pass over until we come to the history of the Hebrews, we come to the following conclusions:—

1. The patriarchal dates were true dates, — astronomic, historic, or geographic, — partly misunderstood by those who recorded them.

2. We can get at the meaning only by penetrating and throwing aside the misconceptions.

3. The Biblical record consists of two versions, — the version of the "Elohim," and the version according to Seth.

4. It begins in a purely ideal statement; but what follows contains reminiscences of thousands of years of primeval life.

5. Hebel, or Abel, the "thing of nought," *vanishing* away, belongs to the ideal sphere. He represents the subjugation of the mild shepherd races by the fierce Kossites, — dwellers in towns, — Turanians descended from Cain.

6. The first epoch in history, therefore, is Turanian, represented in Scripture by the migration of Cain, who went sullenly out to build cities to the east of Eden.

7. Then followed what we may call the Middle Age of that primeval world. Cain left behind him the development of the races. Eastward went the warriors, westward the priests.

8. Then come the descent and predominance of conquering, overbearing Kossite races; its natural result in debauchery; and then the Flood. Great clearness is here thrown into the narrative, by putting the story of Nimrod into its right place, — before the Flood and the dispersion of the Semitic races; and by showing that Nimrod was no Cushite from the South, but a Koshite, or Kossack, a mountaineer, — a conclusion which the books of the Zend justify.

9. Then came the Flood: of its duration we know nothing certainly.

10. Then came the great Semitic emigration, beginning with Heber, the man who "crossed the river," the ancestor of the Hebrews. This emigration may have originated in antediluvian pressure, exerted by Kossite hordes under Nimrod.

11. Almost all nations have some traditions of the Flood, which retain a wonderful harmony. That of Abraham seems nearest to pure history.

12. Abraham's roots are Aryan.

13. The Semites exerted no influence in Egypt, except through the invading Hyksos.

14. The Egyptians, emigrating before the Flood, had no knowledge of it.

15. Vast hordes of Southern Palestinians, driven out of Egypt 1,700 B.C., were the real Pelasgi; in Semitic, *Pelashet*, or wanderers. They drove the Aryans westward, out of the Greek islands. Perhaps the convulsions which drove the Phœnicians from the five cities near the Dead

Sea to the sea-coast, had prepared the way. These emigrations made the channel through which Asiatic ideas were to penetrate the Greek mythology.

From these conclusions, we have the following approximate table of dates:—

    I. Creation of man in Northern Asia . . . . 20,000 B.C.
    II. Flood and geological disturbance . . . . . 10,000 ,,

FIRST AGE.

Antediluvian history. Formation of languages and peoples between the Creation and the Flood.

    I. Sinism (deposited in China) . . . 20,000 to 15,000 B.C.
    II. Old Turanian (in Tartary) . . . 15,000 to 12,000 ,,
    III. Khamism (in Egypt) . . . . . 12,000 to 11,000 ,,

SECOND AGE.

The Flood. Emigration to Egypt.

    IV. The Formation of Semism, and of Nimrod's Turanian kingdom . 10,000 to 7,250 B.C.
    V. Of Iranism in Persia . . . . . 7,250 to 4,000 ,,
    VI. Chaldeeism in Babylon, and the empire of Menes in Egypt . . . . 0,000 to 3,623 ,,

THIRD AGE.

    VII. Of Abraham . . . . . . from 2,877 to 1,320 B.C.
         Of Moses . . . . from 1,320 to 604 ,,

In the first age, Sinism was first deposited in North China. In its language, every syllable was a word, every word a picture. In its worship, the cosmic agencies and the souls of ancestors were adored.

Turanianism deposited itself in Thibet. Its language, like that of the South-American tribes, was a pure agglutination, from which particles soon originated.

Khamism deposited itself in Egypt. The roots and stems of language were formed, and hieroglyphics began.

Then came the Flood; and, just before it or with it, an emigration of Aryans from the regions of the Oxus and Jaxartes, and of Semites from the Euphrates and Tigris.

In the first period of the second age, the Aryans and Semites separate still farther in Asia; the invasion of Nimrod takes place; a watch-tower is built on the plains of Babylon; and the Aryans move into Bactria.

In the second period of the second age, the Aryans gradually separate into Kelts, Armenians, Iranians, Greeks, Sclaves, and Germans. The Northern Semites separate from the Southern, and a central Aryan civilization begins in Asia. The Aryans move to the Indus, the Chaldæans to Babylonia. Zoroaster appears about 3000 B.C. Babylon is built by the son of Belus. Abram is born, and moves toward Mesopotamia.

In the third age, not only does Abraham move into Canaan, but the convulsion in the neighborhood of the Dead Sea drives the inhabitants of the five cities to the coast; and Tyrian chronology begins, and, by astronomic and other synchronistic points, establishes the era.

In the first period of the second age, Egypt forms its "nomes" or provinces, and the republican power in them comes to an end. They have their first priestly king; and then, in the second period, elective kings for 817 years. Then a double government, and the original worship of the sun develops into three forms, — the worship of Seth, of Ra, and of Ammon.

In the third period of the second age, while Babylon is building, history begins in Egypt. Menes is on the throne, and the whole country under one government. The system of writing changes: the hieroglyphic takes on a cursive character, and becomes hieratic. Animal worship begins, and the largest pyramids are built.

In the third age, while the descendants of Abraham are in Canaan, Sesortosis employs Joseph as his "shalith" in Egypt; and, under the pressure of the great famine, the tenure of land is changed throughout Egypt. This put it in the power of the kings to oppress their people. It was according to poetical justice, that, Joseph having advised and consummated this great iniquity, his people, in remote centuries, should smart beneath the power it conferred.

To resume : The first emigration from the Garden is described as moving east; and the emigrants are not shepherds, like Abel, but husbandmen, dwellers in towns. The Turanian language shows the first step; the Khamitic (*i.e.*, the Egyptian), the second. Khamism disappears slowly in Asia; but from the districts about the Euphrates, through Mesopotamia and Palestine, a body of people moved, of whom we know nothing except their language. This language, rediscovered in the "Book of the Dead," speaks to us in syllables that were ancient 4,000 years ago. From this language we discover that the emigration took place before the Flood, and that, by breaking up old ties of race, it opened a new historic consciousness to the emigrants. The shortest line from inorganic language to the organic is through the Chinese, the Turanian, and the later Semitic. But the history of our Iranian languages carries us back to the remotest periods. When the Aryans separated, they already possessed an orderly system of family life. They tended their flocks, practised husbandry, and their language teemed with philosophic germs, with suggestions of mythology. The whole grammatical structure, the terms for designating all family relations, are common to Bactrians, Indians, Greeks, Sclaves, Germans, and Latins. The latest of the grand emigrations was probably that of the Aryans into the Punjaub. Their oldest hymns date from 3000 B.C.; but at that time they had a national existence. Between 10,000 and 4000 B.C., a Semitic development was attained, separate from the Egyptian; an Iranian, separate from the Semitic. That is to say, as the Aryan stream moved westward, it deposited itself first as Iranian, then as

Semitic, then as Egyptian; but the crystallization of this deposit into prior forms of life and government may have been in the inverse order.

The "Ethiops" of the classics lived beyond Syene, where the Nubians now live. They did not speak the Egyptian language, and were governed by kings controlled by priests, — kings who were the tools of that caste. Between the Tigris and Euphrates lived peaceable Semites. In Palestine was a medley of tribes, nomadic and bandit. Egypt was the granary of the world, and the caravan trade still greater than it is now. The influence of Ethiopia upon her in the middle empire was very great. The wife of Amosis, the founder of the new empire, was an Ethiopian heiress; and, although nothing would seem more certain than that Pharaoh was swallowed up with his hosts, what he really did was to flee to Ethiopia, with his son and his gods, in the panic of the Exodus. The civilizing power came into Egypt from Asia. It went first to Upper Egypt, and thence descended to the Delta. The first emperors were Thinites, who came from Abydos to found Memphis. Theban kings were on the throne at the close of the old empire, and during the whole of the middle empire, or Hyksos usurpation. They form the most brilliant element of the new empire which came after; and we find it reflected in the poems of Homer. Memphis was the focus of the old empire. From the twenty-first dynasty, it was the cradle of royal races. The nations of the old world turned towards the Mediterranean, as plants turn towards the light. Alexandria and the great cities of the Delta began to draw vitality from Asia; and Upper Egypt sank into the shade. Egypt was always the child of both Asia and Africa. In Ethiopia, the priest had the upper hand; in Egypt, the warrior. The king whom the Thebans once chose on the Libyan mountain, as Synesius tells, must have been a priest.

All this was over when Menes came to the throne.

Sacerdotal government was the *ultimatum* of Ethiopia. In Egypt, it was only transitional. Only a generation after Joseph made over to the crown the whole fee simple of the country, we find a second Sesortosis building the Labyrinth. When Strabo says that the representatives of each nome, or province, assembled there, at the great festival of the Panegyries, he transmits its history. At Thebes, every vestige of the early freedom was now destroyed. The independence of the nomes was lost in the gigantic building, the monster of imperial power, that devoured freedom.

The following tables will give a bird's-eye view of the development of Egypt:—

PRIOR TO MENES.

I. Rule of sacerdotal kings in the Thebaid, Bytis.
II. Elected kings in the Thebaid. Last Ethiopic constitution.
III. Hereditary princes. Confederation in two groups. Asiatic influence prevailing.
IV. Double empire. National civilization.
V. Predominance of Lower-Egypt and Asiatic ideas.

FROM MENES TO THE LOSS OF INDEPENDENCE.

I. Unity of empire under the first dynasty.
II. Decline of the Thinite line, re-action towards Ethiopia, worship of animals becoming national, under the 2d, 3d, and 4th dynasties.
III. Separation. The 5th (Theban) dynasty gives way to the 6th (Memphite).
IV. Separation into two governments. Conquered Memphites disappear in the 8th dynasty. The North revolts. At Pelusium, a way is opened for Asia to prevail, when the Sesostridæ at Thebes become extinct.
V. The power of the Pharaohs becomes restricted to the Thebaid. They form marriage connections in Ethiopia. In dynasties 13, 14, and 17, the Ethiopian element becomes fixed.
VI. The Thebans restore the empire. Theban kings reign down to the 20th dynasty.

VII. A Re-action. The Thebans die out. Princely houses of the Delta, especially the Saite, furnish the kings for the 21st and the 26th dynasty.
VIII. The Ethiopians dethrone Bochoris the Reformer, and reign fifty years as the 25th dynasty.
IX. Supremacy of the Asiatic element shows itself throughout the reign of Psammetichus of Sais. Egypt is in friendly relations with Greece. Its great bodies of feudal soldiery are breaking up.
X. It is subjugated by Persia, and later by Macedonia.

At the risk of seeming repetition, we must give one more tabular view, to indicate the position of Egypt as regards the development of civilization and government. The last table showed what races swayed her, what divisions of races occurred within her own limits. We divide the story now into five epochs, indicated in outline below. Our object is to show, that a very much longer period of time was needed for her development than has been hitherto accorded.

First Epoch, 1,500 years. — Egypt's primeval time; the formation of language; the development of the Khamitic character, language, and picture-writing. Latest point, 9500 B.C.

Second Epoch, 2,000 years. — Transition period; formation of mythology; age of Egyptian idiographic characters, up to syllableism; development of the worship of Osiris. Latest point, 8000 B.C.

Third Epoch, 1,100 years. — Political commencement; formation of the nomes; constitution of districts; formation of a system of phonetics; hieroglyphs, with syllables up to the alphabet. Latest point, 7000 B.C.

Fourth Epoch, 1,500 years. — Double government, Upper and Lower Egypt; formation of a constitution and an alphabet. Latest point, 5500 B.C.

Fifth Epoch. — This begins with the reign of Menes, in

historic order, at 3400 B.C., which gives us a chronology like this: —

Khamism, forming into a nation	1,500 years.
Osirism and picture-writing developing	1,500 ,,
Formation of the nomes	1,500 ,,
Consolidation of Upper and Lower Egypt	1,500 ,,
Both united in religion under Menes	3,400 B.C.
Which carries history back to	9,400 B.C.

This gives us 6,000 years before Menes. It can be proved, that, at his accession, language, manners, and religion had already become rigid. There were, before his time, we are told, 180 generations, which gives us 5,400 years; and we must throw the emigration back of the Flood, of which it preserved no tradition. That this is not an extravagant estimate, we shall see; for Manetho gives 5,212 human princes before Menes. If we throw out the usual proportion of contemporaneous kings, still this period is not too long.

We shall indicate in what manner, in Bunsen's view, the existence and antiquity of all other Asiatic nations are involved in that of Egypt. It has been impossible to pause to prove the positions taken. The proof is found in following the two subordinate branches of the main inquiry, — the Hebrew chronology, and the history of the Egyptian literature and monuments, in which we have found the chief interest of these volumes. The scheme of the 21,000-years' cycle is illustrated by careful plates, drawn, in accordance with ancient and modern observation, under the direction of a skilful astronomer. The Sothiac festive year, it will be readily acknowledged, was of such importance, that its celebration would always be remembered in connection with the king reigning at the time of its celebration. If we celebrated the fourth of July only once in a hundred years, of course the President in office at the time would become prominent. There must be 1,461 years between any two reigns in which such an event occurred: so we have a regulator for the internal chronology. A careless reader might find no proof of the assertion, that Nimrod was a Kossite [Koshite or Kossack], or mountaineer of the Caucasus. The proof is mixed in with the philological investigations, and is to be found in the enumerations of the Zend.

The reader who has attempted Bunsen, and given up its perusal in despair, may doubt the fairness of any exposition of his work which seems to run smoothly. It seems proper, then, to indicate in what manner our statement has been prepared. It is based upon the conclusions of the first four volumes of "Egypt's Place in History," carefully studied out and compared. Whatever changes are suggested (if any) in the fifth volume are to be further treated by themselves; for that part of it which does not consist of Egyptian remains is merely a summing-up of results. In this reduction, we have thrown out all technical learning not essential to the reader's comprehension of the subject. Learning, necessary to Bunsen's own preparation for his work, is frequently bewildering to the student, who looks chiefly for results. We have also suppressed all variations in the spelling, which grow out of philological habits. Common readers are puzzled when Ham suddenly becomes Chem; or Iranian, Aryan. As Bunsen's work was gradual, and his inquiry progressive, dates are assumed in his first volume, which are slightly changed in the fourth. He has a way, too, of mentioning dates, sometimes in a specific and sometimes in an approximate way, which is puzzling. Thus he sometimes speaks of the culmination of favorable influences, in the thirteenth century of our era, as having occurred in 1240, sometimes as in 1248. Such variations as arise from the development of his work have a real value in the book itself, because they show when and how his conclusions are affected; but they have no such value to the general reader. They only confuse him with their uncertainty. We adhere, therefore, to the specific dates.

It is not likely that we have been able to assume these changes without making some mistakes; but better incur the blame of that, than permit this magnificent work to be wholly obscured and hidden by inconsistencies so trivial.

We take little note, so far, of the new conclusions in Bunsen's fifth and last volume. In the first place, the five months which have elapsed since the publication are not time sufficient for the profound study which his book requires; in the second, we fail to see the force of the reasoning which induced him at the last to yield to the old Alexandrian chronology, — to yield, too, when every thing seemed to favor his more extended scheme. It is a very delicate and true scholarship which is fitted to deal with this question and the new conclusion which forces the whole history of Egypt into a period five hundred years later, and presses, as it seems to us, several things out of fit place. But we will conclude these notes by some extracts from this volume, of a kind suited to the student who means to study it in earnest.

The Epilogue is divided, problems and key into four parts, each consisting of nine principal heads: —

I. Results as to chronological problems exclusively Egyptian.

II. Chronological results connected with synchronisms, — Biblical, Assyrian, Babylonian, and Greek.

III. Results connected with the reconstruction of the ancient ante-chronological but epochal history of Egypt.

IV. Corollaries, philosophical and practical.

The synchronisms are the test of the Egyptian dates; the concordance of Egypt and Asia is the test of the position assigned to the Egyptian language and religion. Finally, the bearing of the historical conclusions upon the reconstruction of universal history is the test of the value of the research.

The date established for the New Empire from Amos to Nectanebo II., 1,294 years, is essentially the date of Manetho, and is sufficiently tested, being supported by *two* absolute dates. These last are found to be historical, by the check of the monuments. It was anciently reported that Manetho's dates depended on the Sothiac cycle. His dates were not arranged in epochs of 1,460 years; but it is impossible to assign any reason for his closing his first and second books with the 11th and 19th Dynasties, except an attempt to conform them to the close of the cycle, in the intercalary, or 1461st year. In Menephtah's case the following cycle took his name, as, in all the known eras of Europe and Asia, cycles have taken the name of the monarchs in whose reign they began.

All the accounts of Greek historians and chronographers, before Manetho, are based on the Egyptian folly of regnal years. As Manetho raised the chronology of the Old and Middle Empires, Eratosthenes and Apollodorus reduced it. The chronological series of the Old Empire from Menes to Amuntimaios, officially examined by Eratosthenes, corrects Manetho as to the Old Empire. It solves all the problems of the first six Dynasties and their equivalents on the tablets of Karnak and Abydos. Eratosthenes and Apollodorus combined give the key to the fundamental error, and, by a second absolute date, confirm Bunsen's chronology.

Of the Alexandrian chronology, he says, —

"It is, in the first place, the *highest* authority. It is of one piece, without heterogeneous elements, and with no gap to fill up. It comes nearest to the Bible dates. Its lists bear a constant analogy to Manetho."

The 215 years of bondage in Egypt form an historical date, according to an official inscription of Tuthmosis III. himself. This Tuthmosis was the fighter who made Nineveh pay tribute, began the oppression, and, not content with his own glory, erased his *sister's* escutcheons. Hence the following important table:—

	B.C.
The first year of Tuthmosis III., an *absolute* date	1574
Time when the Hyksos finally evacuated Egypt	1548
Twelve years in Asia, and Mesopotamia conquered from	1546 to 1534
The Exodus in the fifth year of Menepthah	1320

The bondage began under Tuthmosis III., in the year before his last campaign, 1535 B.C. It is chiefly associated, however, with the memory of his successor, Menepthah.

The journey of Abraham into Egypt occurred toward the close of the 21st century B.C., when the Nantefs ruled. We have papyri of that era which prove an advanced civilization. The great pyramids had been built for many centuries; so had the temple of Ptah, the sanctuary at Memphis. Abraham saw the rich corn-fields, which have in all ages supplied the wants of Kanaan.

As all Egyptologists are not, like Bunsen, general historians, and most historians are ignorant of Egyptology, there exists great ignorance of the nature of Hyksos sway in Egypt. What Manetho states, the monuments confirm. The Shepherds were military nomads, who left Egyptian life quite undisturbed. They never occupied Upper Egypt; but, driving back the native princes, took tribute from them. The forty years, between the Exodus and the passage of the Jordan, are checked and confirmed by an Assyrian and Egyptian date. Happy are those persons, but not to be envied, who have no misgivings about making Moses march out with more than two millions of people, at the end of a popular conspiracy and rising, in the sunny days of the 18th Dynasty; who make the Israelites conquer Kanaan under Joshua, during, and just previously to, the most formidable campaigns of conquering Pharaohs in that same country: The Exodus could have taken place only under Menepthah; and Joshua could not have crossed the Jordan before Easter, 1280 B.C., — the last campaign of Raamses III. having been in 1281; and, at this time, the Jewish Commonwealth must have been already in a state of dissolution under Semiramis, who is no myth, but a perfectly historical personage. The Assyrian dates, found for her, tally with the Egyptian for the 20th Dynasty. Assyria was created by the power of the Ninyads, between 1250 and 1120.

Before Moses, that is before 3500 B.C., there were four epochs: —

I. Epoch of hereditary princes; those of Abydos being prominent.

II. Epoch of elective princes in the nomes; the electors being the priests and nobles.

III. Epoch of sacerdotal kings. The electors the same; the democratic element — *i.e.*, the trades — not yet divided into castes.

IV. Epoch of municipal institutions, with established worship, and a common language in the nomes.

The civilizing element in Egypt seems to have been Osirism, which had its root in Asia. The leading myth of the dying and reviving divinity — symbol of the God-consciousness of the human soul, itself symbolized by the solar year — is not only Asiatic, but so is the etymology of the names, " Isis," " Osiris," " Set." Every thing points to Phœnicia, and from Phœnicia back to Chaldea. The Egyptian language contains deposited germs, which have since developed, sometimes as Semitic, sometimes as Aryan. We find the same roots and stems in the oldest Turanian forms, and these again presuppose a purely substantial language. We should be obliged to assume such a language, did we not find it in the ancient Chinese.

There are various proofs of the antiquity of the sacred

literature of Egypt. The text of the Papyrus of Turin, published by Lepsius, seems to belong to the eighteenth or nineteenth century. In his introduction to the "Book of the Dead," Dr. Birch mentions, as a proof of antiquity, the text of chap. 54 engraved on the statue which the old oppressor, Tuthmosis III., erected to his nurse; and the astounding fact, that chap. 17 is inscribed on the coffin of a queen of the 11th dynasty! 2800 B.C.

Four thousand five hundred years old, at the least, the text agrees entirely with the printed Turin Papyrus.

This seventeenth chapter consists of prayers, addressed to Osiris, the Western Sun, symbol of the uncreated Cause. The glosses on the ancient text prove that it was then nearly unintelligible to the scribes! Here is the hymn of Osiris, Son of God: —

"I am the sun in its setting, the only Being in the Firmament.

I am the rising sun.

The sun's power begins when he is set (*i.e.*, the soul's).

I am the great God. begotten by himself: I can never be stopped by the elementary powers; I am the morning (*i.e.*, resurrection). I know the gate (*i.e.*, of death). The Father of the Spirit, the eternal Soul of the Sun, has examined him and proved him: he has found that the departed fought. on earth, the battle of the Good Gods, as his father, the Lord of Invisible Worlds, had ordered him to do.

I know the Great God, who is invisible.

I am that Phœnix in Heliopolis, always rising again.

I am God, the Creator."

The origin of these hymns is before Menes, and they show the connection of ancestral worship with the worship of the Gods; for, in the chamber of Tuthmosis, the oppressor, the first of the king's sixty ancestors is Ra, or Helios himself.

The Conventional Epoch, of about 4000 B.C., as the beginning of human existence, happens to be, with approximate accuracy, the starting-point of chronological history: —

	B.C.
The era of Babylonian empire is	3784
The era of Menes (Alexandrian?)	3059
The Exodus occurred	1320
The first Olympian year of Rome, and Nabonassar at Babylon is	776–664
Time of Isaiah	740
Jeremiah, Greek philosophy, and Solon, flourished	600
Buddha, Confucius, and Laotsi, about	550
Rome was a republic	500
Socrates lived	400

To return from the general survey, the monuments 2800 B.C. are full of ritualistic formulæ. To feed the hungry, give drink to the thirsty, to clothe the naked and bury the dead, to serve the king loyally, were the first duties of the pious man. Joseph found these commands and the immortality of the soul cut into the pyramids, when he went into Egypt.

In reference to papyri, Dr. Birch says: —

"Rituals are as trustworthy as the best classical manuscripts of the Middle Ages. Like other objects of the funeral equipments, ready-made papyri were always on sale, blank spaces being left for the name of the purchaser, inserted in another hand. In many hieratic papyri, the whole was prepared to order, as the execution shows. Owing to ignorance or carelessness, the titles, vignettes, or rubrics were often omitted."

The books are expressly stated to have been written by "the finger of the Great God."* The principal ideas connected with the ritual are the living after death, the being "born again like the Sun," and the wiping out of "all corruption from the heart."

---

* An explanation of the expression in our Scripture, with reference to the tables of stone; that is, they are of as divine authority as the law in Egypt. — C. H. D.

The mystery of names, the knowledge of which was a sovereign virtue, appears to have existed, not only in Egypt, but elsewhere. Traces of it are found in the Cabbala, the spurious Gospels, and early Roman history, in which the secret name of the city was one of the fatal things. The eleventh chapter of the "Book of the Dead" has also some connection with masonic ordinances, in which the mystical names of the various parts of the doorway are actually found in the Egyptian formulæ, so far as can be gathered from the hints on subjects so removed from popular knowledge.

Considered as a whole, this ritual is the most important of the texts, as regards the variety of information that it gives. The Deities referred to are either Solar or Infernal. Like all Oriental writings, its mysteries are conveyed in allegorical language, the principal persons being alluded to by epithets or qualifications. The style is concise, and straightforward, and for the most part without any metrical flow.

From its pages we copy one or two things that strike us as we turn them over:—

"I am Yesterday, the Morning, the Light at its birth the second time, the Mystery of the Soul, made by the gods."

"I am the Inundator. Great Listener is thy name." (The words also stand for the Nile and Egypt.)

"I am the Lord of Life. I have come forth from the great gate. I have rejoined the eye."

"He does all that he chooses, like the gods there, in garments of truth, for ever" (or "millions of times").*

"He will go to the gods who belong to the Sun, for he has stood at the boat of the Sun in the course of every day."—"When this is done, his Soul lives for ever; he does not die again in Hades. He is not annihilated when words are weighed. His word is good against his enemies; his food is off the table of the Sun."

* See a similar use of numbers in our Scripture. — C. H. D.

Osiris is as well spoken (*i.e.*, speaks as well?) on earth as in Hades. Humanity is so essential, that there are twenty-one "Gates of the Meek-hearted"! The name of one doorkeeper is "Upsetter of Forms." Greatly must it have rejoiced the heart of the ancient Egyptian to know it. The name of another was "Stopper of the Verbose." Bores, then, were of ancient institution! Many passages recall to us formulæ in the Psalms of David.

In the inscriptions, the scribe Mentusa says, "I never repeated an evil word." Long be his name remembered! Another says, "I injured no child; I oppressed no widow. There was no beggar in my days: I made the widow like the woman with an husband." The text of Raamses II., about the Hebrews, says, "I have heard the message which my Lord sent, saying, Give corn to the men and soldiers and Hebrews, who are drawing the stone to fortify the place of Raamses, the living, delivered to the general of militia, Ameneman. I have given them corn every month, according to the instruction of my Lord." *Apiuruiu* is the word for Hebrews.

In examining the great work of Lepsius, one is struck by great resemblances to remains in Central Asia. The gold crosses on the priest's dresses identify the caste. A lion sits beside the king, whose throne-name shows that he is only a vicegerent. P. H. Ra, is Pharaoh, or the Sun. A Hawk is a prophecy of the Phœnix; and the Sun itself indicates the royal banners. The Princes fanned the King, or carried his palanquin: a peculiar lock of hair, uncut, also indicates their subordinate position. To the sacred architecture and painting, perspective was forbidden; reminding one of the Mosaic formula, "Thou shalt not make unto thee any likeness of any thing that is in heaven above, or in the earth beneath," &c. Idols are seen, filled with barley, which of course their priests consumed. At the feet of the king, the tongues, ears, and phalli of the conquered peoples are piled up. Glue is used in every age. The sandstone walls, coated with lime to color, are carefully protected from the rain, a deep groove (V) is cut where the stones of the roof unite; and a wider stone is fitted carefully in, with broad, projecting eaves.

PART II.

EGYPTIAN HISTORY, AS A FRAMEWORK TO HEBREW CHRONOLOGY.

HAVING shown the shallowness of Bunsen's critics, the character of his own preparation and life, and given a general view of the place Egypt filled in history, according to his investigations, we now propose to show, in detail, the internal history of Egypt, and the manner in which the Hebrew chronology depends upon, and illustrates it. We condense as far as the desire to be intelligible will permit, and refer students of *proof in detail* to the volumes themselves.

The first recorded king of Egypt was Menes; and, from his time to that of Alexander, the history of Egypt is divided into three periods: —

1. The *Old Empire*, beginning with Menes . . . . 3643 B.C. and lasting 1,076 years, to the end of the Thirteenth Dynasty.
2. The *Middle Empire*, beginning with the Fourteenth Dynasty . . . . 2567 B.C. and lasting 928 years. Convulsed by Hyksos' disturbance, and ending with the Seventeenth Dynasty.
3. The *New Empire*, which began with the vigorous Eighteenth Dynasty . . . . 1626 B.C. and was an attempt to revive the fortunes of Egypt under the families of Raamses and Amosis.

In the *Old Empire*, the names of Menes, Sesostris, Amenema, and Mencheres are prominent. In the *Middle Empire*, we find usurpers, none of whom were important. In the *New Empire*, we have various sovereigns of the house of Raamses, confounded frequently with the Sesortosidæ, of the Old Empire, in common tradition.

We had hoped to proceed to the Hebrew chronology, connected with the discussion of our subject, without showing, in greater detail, the vicissitudes of the Egyptian throne; but this proves to be impossible. The theories of Bunsen, sustained we think by monumental evidence, are wholly different from those of Brugsch, discussed lately in the book notices of the "Examiner." According to Bunsen, a much longer period than five hundred years is necessary to account for the growth of the Hebrew nation; and the Semitic kings left no more traces of themselves upon the monuments of Egypt, than upon the desert sands their invading feet had crossed. We remind our readers, then, that *Thirty Dynasties* complete the historic record of Egypt, and that for these thirty Bunsen is able to account; but they are not put upon record in their numerical order, that order consisting of the mistaken inferences of old writers. The monuments prove that they did not succeed each other, but were often cotemporaneous; and that, in times of internecine war, the old lists frequently put the struggling princes into the line of descent, as if they were father and son, instead of lord and rebel. To give some idea of the succession of princes must, then, be our first work, — the greatest difficulty encountered in the work of restoration appertaining, of course, to the *Old Empire*.

The *First Dynasty* was Thinite, and consisted of five kings. This era Bunsen places between 4000 and 2800 B.C.; and it would seem, from recent decisions in reference to the age of the Great Pyramid, as if the older date were most likely to be true.

Menes, the first king, reigned over both countries, 3643 B.C., and found a matured civilization. He regulated the course of the Nile, improved its western arm, and drained the nome of Memphis so that the city of that name could be built. His influence was religious and distinct. The succeeding kings made themselves famous in medicine and mathematics. Physicians still use the Egyptian signs for drachms and grains, and mark their recipes with the sacred sign of a planet in its contracted form. Our numerals also are Egyptian, to which India added the cipher. The last king of this dynasty Bunsen marks as a "Heraclide," perhaps the progenitor of the Greek family. The pyramids of Kokomi were also built. Then, perhaps because of a royal marriage, the line divides, and —

The *Second Dynasty* and the *Third* are on two thrones, at This and Memphis, 3453 B.C. Here the lists bear an interesting testimony in reference to the age and size of man : for the first king of the second dynasty is mentioned as a giant, eight feet nine inches tall, who built the pyramids at Ghizeh; and the generations averaged, six thousand years ago, exactly as they do to-day. In these dynasties, females were admitted to the throne, — a fruitful source of confusion afterward. To this was soon added another, — the spiteful habit of erasing the escutcheons of preceding kings, after family divisions or civil wars. In the second and third dynasties, animal worship took the place of a cosmical and astral faith, writing became cursive, a system of castes began, and the brick pyramids at Dashoor and Abouseer were built. Then, too, the Nile ran honey for eleven days.

Under the *Fourth Dynasty*, the empire was united again for 155 years (3229 B.C.). It began with the Cheops of Herodotus, the builder of the Great Pyramid. Compulsory labor began; but Mencheres, the holy, abolished it, and restored the old and purer religion.

Then came cotemporaneously the *Fifth and Sixth Dynasties*, — the fifth consisting of one man, a usurper, Othoes, who founded the tormenting and confusing line of Heracleapolitan kings, and was killed by his own guards.

The *Sixth Dynasty* opened with the wonderful reign of Phiops Apappus, 3074 B.C. He was crowned at six years of age, and reigned a hundred years, — as great a wonder then as it would be now. His son, and after that his son's widow, Nitocris, reigned *with* this old man. *She* put her husband's murderer to death; and with her, 5,000 years ago, the pretty story of *Cinderella* originated. She had been a slave; and one day, while she was bathing, the wind carried her slipper to the king, who would not rest till he had found her. With the grandchildren of old Phiops came a confused period.

The *Seventh, Eighth, Ninth, Tenth,* and *Eleventh Dynasties* were then upon the throne together, 2915 B.C. The race of Phiops continued on the throne at Memphis as the seventh and eighth. The eleventh, composed of a Theban family, — the Nantefs, — reigned at Thebes; and the ninth and tenth were in the Delta, near Pelusium. Here the glory of Memphis ends. The Theban family of Nantefs, whose monuments, coffins, gilded bodies, and votive tablets still exist to tell the story, comes up again in the twelfth dynasty with the Sesostridæ. Arabs ravaged the grand old city; and the native princes, who kept their thrones, began to pay the Hyksos tribute.

With this *Twelfth Dynasty* the glory of the Old Empire rose to its height. The first Sesostris, 2754 B.C., created the fertile nome of the Fayoum, by filling a rocky basin with Nile mud; its magnificent drains, dams, and gates still challenging the brains of the archæologist. He conquered all the land, from Cush to the copper mines of Sinai. His tombs have Doric columns. His statue is now at Berlin. In the reign of his son, Sesostris II., we find fine colored sculpture, chess-playing, and glass-blowing. Sesostris III. made canals, built forts, and conquered Europe to Thrace. Mares, his son (?), built the Labyrinth, in which the provinces were afterwards convened, and Lake Mœris. Under

Sesostris I., the second king of this family, Joseph went down into Egypt, and Jacob emigrated. In his "Bible Work," Bunsen fixes this date at 2747 B.C., which gives nearly 1,400 years for the development of the Hebrew nation. The monuments show that it was no uncommon thing for such immigrations to take place. Driven by famine, war, or local distresses, bands of Arabs came down, were received, and devoted themselves to the care of the king's flocks. Such communities, doubtless, swelled the "mixed multitude" of the Exodus. The Scripture indicates very distinctly that the king whom Joseph knew was no Bedawin or Hyksite. An inscription in Upper Egypt records the terrible famine which the Hebrew viceroy relieved; and connected with the reign of this Sesostris was that change in the tenure of the soil which added to the oppressions of the people, and is recorded in Gen. xlvii. 20-26. It would seem, then, that we have here a fixed synchronistic point; and there can be no dispute, except about the length of the interval between this king and the Menepthah of the Exodus. The wise reign of Sesostris, intended to avert national ruin, was followed by a period of victory and prosperity. Sesostris found the empire under the control of three or four Dynasties. The kings in the Delta had once grasped imperial power. When the building of the splendid monuments at Syene was followed by the grand erection of the Labyrinth, and the more useful creation of Lake Mœris, then popular hatred rose to its height.

The kings in the Delta hated the Labyrinth, — a perpetual reminder of their own inferiority, because intended to accommodate the princes who came up to pay tribute, — and helped to destroy it. They made use of religious differences to create discontent, — an easy task where one province worshipped the crocodile, and another the ichneumon, its natural destroyer. The treachery of the Delta brought in the invading Hyksos without a blow.

From the *Twelfth to the Seventeenth Dynasty*, desolation and confusion reigned. Native monuments—among others, the tablet of the dead at Gurnah—represent the native kings as tributary to the Hyksos down to the time of the eighteenth dynasty; but the Arab has not perpetuated here the memory of his usurpation: we find it only in the remote legends of his wandering race. In Arabia, they say, the Shepherds ruled eight hundred years in Egypt. The proof of Manetho's Hyksos chronology lies in the evidence, that upon no other assumption can the second Sothiac cycle fall in the eleventh dynasty. All scholars admit that the third fell in the nineteenth.

The *Eighteenth Dynasty* of Theban kings makes us familiar with the names of Amosis, Tuthmosis, and Amenophis. It opens with the reign of the wonderful Amos, who drove out the Shepherds, and had a lovely Ethiop wife, whose name meant "fair and blameless," in accordance with the old Homeric suggestion. A very striking portrait of her was once shown by Professor Lesly, at the Lowell Institute. From her time, no honor could be conferred on an Egyptian woman so great as the being permitted to bear her name. A daughter of Amos and this Aahmes-Nefruari built Cleopatra's Needle; but one of her brothers afterward enviously erased her escutcheons. Three of her brothers built at Karnak and Tetmes. The statue called Memnon by the Greeks was really a statue erected, in this glorious *Eighteenth Dynasty*, to the great conqueror, Tuthmosis III., a son of Amos and the beautiful Nefruari. It was erected by his own grandson, and the mistake grew out of the misapprehension of the Egyptian word for "monument,"— **mem-nen.** The young Amenophis, who created the *mem-nen*, was a heretic, worshipping the visible disc of the sun. He built the palace of Luxor.

His grandfather, Tuthmosis III., had a history which may be thus summed up:—

He forced the Shepherds to evacuate Suez in . . . . 1548 B.C.
Made a campaign, and was victorious over Nineveh and
  Babylon, in . . . . 1546 „
Employed the Jews in building, so that the period of
  oppression may be said to have begun in . . . . 1534 „

Might he not have been content to leave untouched the escutcheons of his sister, Mespres, which he enviously destroyed?

The *Nineteenth Dynasty* teems with warlike expeditions into Barbary and Crete, and magnificent erections of temples, obelisks, and fortresses. Its six kings, beginning to reign about 1450 B.C., all bear familiar names. They are called Sethos or Raamses, with one exception,— the fanatic of the Exodus, whose name was Menepthah. The heresy of the young Amenophis spread. The whole country was in confusion. Raamses II., who reigned from 1391 to 1325 B.C., — a date positively ascertained, — was the first consistent oppressor of the Jews. There is a signet-ring of his, which the child Moses may have played with. His portrait is now at Memphis. There was some ground for the popular hatred of the Jews, and the royal abuse of them. The people could remember a time before Joseph, when they had land of their own. The king, a fanatic, trying to make amends for heresies, believed that their presence in the country offended the gods. *Menepthah* followed Raamses II.; and in his reign occurred the Exodus. The remains of this period, in an artistic point of view, are extremely beautiful. The most finished papyri in the world Moses might have carried, and possibly did carry, beyond Jordan. Menepthah was a weak fanatic. The hatred of the people for Raamses, who had overtasked Egyptians as well as Jews, was so great, that his son could never finish his tomb. Menepthah yielded, Manetho tells us, to a "revolt of lepers." Not so fortunate as to be drowned in the Red Sea, which swallowed up his host, he fled to Ethiopia, with his heir and his sacred bull, and remained there until his son was old enough to recover the kingdom. When Moses went out of Egypt, there were two claimants of the throne, beside Menepthah, — Sipthah and Amen-Messu. Does not this give some meaning to the king's fear, that, if the Jews stayed, they might unite with his enemies? Sipthah was married, in infancy, to Tauser, the sister of Menepthah, and daughter of Raamses the oppressor. One of Sipthah's inscriptions is a prayer, beseeching Heaven for children to inherit the throne. Was Tauser the princess who, despairing of issue by her boy-husband, begged of the stern old Raamses the lovely babe she found in the bulrushes? The character of the times makes it easy to see what position Moses might have held in that court, and recalls the appeal of Satan in the temptation, "All these things will I give thee, if thou wilt fall down, and worship me :" one of the many analogies discoverable in the lives of Moses and Jesus.

The *Twentieth Dynasty*, still Theban, opens with the name of a mean fellow, named Marres Phruores, whose precise relationship to Menepthah is not clear. He found nothing better to do than to put his own throne-mark on older monuments, and suggest to the Greeks the god Proteus. His son was Raamses III., a magnificent conqueror, whose splendid tomb contains a painted sea-fight. His beautiful red granite coffin is at Paris ; its lid at Cambridge, England. It was in the fourteenth year of this king, that Joshua crossed the Jordan. His conquests in Palestine had compelled the Jews to refrain from entering Canaan up to that time. He was succeeded by ten kings, who all bore the name of Raamses. The eighth of these was the last who carried the god Set on his escutcheon. With the extinction of the Ramessidæ, a great revolution occurred.

The *Twenty-First Dynasty*, containing seven kings, consisted of a priestly caste who had at last got the better of the struggling heretics.

Nine Bubastite kings constitute the *Twenty-Second Dynasty*. The first of these was Shishak. In the front court at Karnak is the sculpture which shows how he treated Rehoboam at Jerusalem, — the "Bible Work" says in 968 B.C.

In the *Twenty-Third Tanite Dynasty*, we have four strange kings.

In the *Twenty-Fourth Dynasty*, one Saite, in whose reign (Bocchoris's) "a lamb spoke." The people received from him peace and a constitutional government.

In the *Twenty-Fifth Dynasty*, three Ethiops reigned.

In the *Twenty-Sixth Dynasty*, we have nine Saite kings, two of them known to us in the Scripture. The fifth of them, Necho II., defeated Josiah at Megiddo, and took Jerusalem, 607 B.C. Two years after, he was defeated in his turn by Nebuchadnezzar. The next but one who succeeded him was the Hofra of Scripture, properly Uaphres.

The *Twenty-Seventh Dynasty* records the Persian rule from Cambyses to Darius II.

The *Twenty-Eighth*, *Twenty-Ninth*, and *Thirtieth*, only an obscure succession of Saites, Mendesians, and Sebennytes; eight kings in all.

This is the scaffolding which is to sustain the walls of the historic erection we are contemplating.

SYNCHRONISMS.

Starting from well-established facts, we find various fixed points of synchronism between Egyptian monuments and Asiatic history. Calculating upwards, we fail to find any thing certain in the Hebrew records, until the 10th century before Christ. From Egyptian monuments we obtain the date of Moses, and conclude that the Exodus took place under the Pharaoh whose name is attached to the last imperial canicular cycle. We have also fixed the age of Joseph, who was minister of Sesortosen of the *Twelfth Dynasty.*

From this we work upwards, on critical grounds, to the period when Abraham emerged from Chaldea. Abraham's date is 2870 B.C., 750 years after the reign of Menes began. Between the two, we have important monuments; and there are synchronistic points down to the time of Joseph.

Regular chronology began with Menes. His reign consolidated Upper and Lower Egypt into one empire; but it began when civilization was mature, and with registers of previous reigns, which must, at the very least, have stretched through 5,500 years. It had already language, written character, and a completed mythos.

Down to the lowest time, the Pharaohs were called Lords of the Upper and Lower country. The government was based on twenty-seven Nomes; ten belonging to the upper country, ten to the lower, and seven constituting the heptanomys, or Central Egypt. These Nomes were the independent bases of all democratic Egyptian life. Their existence was opposed to the despotic element in the later empire. With Menes, they possessed much power and many privileges.

The Labyrinth was the temple and the tomb of their latest liberty; yet, even under the New Empire, every province had its own capital, shrine, and peculiar privileges. The formation of these twenty-seven Nomes, which was consummated before chronology begins, must have occupied a large part of the 5,500 years before Menes. It was a stage of life posterior to the family and the patriarchal; and a strong bond of common language and religion originally held them together.

The language and people of China may be older than those of Egypt; but the regular chronology of Egypt goes back to 5,000 years before Christ, an advantage enjoyed by no other nation.

The Chinese have no traditions of the great flood. The *cycle of sixty years*, which the Chinese use, is a primitive institution, and the key to their whole astronomical system. The old Indian cycles began with one of five years, probably multiplied by twelve. This was the Chinese way. To find the time when the solar and lunar year started together, takes us back to 2375 B.C. The present notation of the months only goes back to 2000 B.C. There the *real* history begins. The Chinese used the old Babylonian gnomon. The inundation in the reign of Tao had no more to do with Noah's flood than the canals!

The world's history is the development of two races and two languages, — the Semitic and the Iranian. For the Egyptian is only the African deposit of a very early form of the Semitic, in which the Semitic germs are organized. We can link the Egyptian to the Chinese and the Turanian: we expect, therefore, to find some connection between their mythologies.

People who say there is no authority for certain conclusions, forget that language is the very best of authority. Egypt represents the real middle age of the world. It is the chrysalis of primeval Asia, in which a new life begins to stir. This Semitic branch stretched through Menes, even to the Mediterranean, and obtained positive rank in the world. It struggled on in antagonism to the land and race from which it had sprung. Both fell under the Aryans, who keep the throne of the world to this day. Egypt yielded first to the Persian branch of the Aryans. Cyrus conquered the Medes and Bactrians; and, by taking Babylon, subjected all Semitic nations to himself. But it was Alexander, the great European Aryan, who severed for ever the thread of Egyptian life.

Renan denies the affinity between the language and religion of Egypt and Asia, which Bunsen asserts; but reiterates Bunsen's assertion, when he admits elsewhere the identity of Coptic and Semitic pronouns. The Bible is on the side of Bunsen. Ham is the father of Canaan; and it was the Semitic language of the Canaanites which the descendants of Abraham adopted. Those Canaanites, driven back from Egypt, became themselves the Pelasgi (Coptic, Pelashet), or *wanderers* of the world. Modern history begins with Abraham.

CONCLUSIONS.

1. There is an historical connection between Greek mythology, the primeval Bible record, and the oldest religions of Egypt and Asia.
2. The religion of Egypt is merely the mummy of the religion of Central Asia; the deposit of the oldest mythology on African soil.
3. Primeval Asia is the starting point for us and them.
4. The Greeks did not invent their mythology; they only humanized it.
5. Moses adopted no ideas from Egypt which had not an older common source in Asia. The Bible contains no conscious mythology. Any personification of Divine ideas is foreign to its intention.
6. The popular sentiment reflected in the Bible had its root nevertheless in old mythologic times.
7. The personal history of the Jews begins with Abraham; but many of the ancient traditions which he brought out from a mythological people clung to him and to Isaac and Jacob, were interwoven with the story of their lives, and influenced them to idolatry from the time of the Exodus to that of the Captivity.

CONCLUSIONS IN REGARD TO LANGUAGE.

1. Language develops quietly; but, in the end, its central stem is so modified that the oldest and the newest

forms cannot hold intelligible communion with each other, any more than with their offshoots.

2. Foreign words may come into its dictionary, but not into its grammar.

3. Every stage of such a language, becoming more affluent in words, becomes poorer in its grammar.

4. The Iranian languages, from India to Iceland and Lithuania, are identical in grammar and roots, as also are among themselves the different Semitic forms. Every Chinese word is a root, which may be a noun or a verb, according to its position; consequently it is not yet an individualized stem. There was an interval of a thousand years between Charlemagne (the first king of the Germans), and Francis II. (the last); and they both belonged to the same race. The art of writing existed in the time of Charlemagne, and German civilization has never been violently broken up; but these two persons could not understand each other if they were now to meet.

These are the philological principles which assist in the development of the oldest chronologies, and which are to be borne in mind throughout our whole discussion.

It is an unsatisfactory way to begin to write history in the middle; but this is necessary to indicate, in a general way, Egypt's position in the great tide of dividing immigrating races.

It is seen, then, that her civilization threw a bridge from Asia into Europe; and, standing upon it, we look "before and after." We believe with Bunsen, that the Hebrew residence in the Delta was of long duration; that seventy souls went down with Jacob into Egypt, was a steadfast tradition. The Egyptians counted "bonds-people" among the "goods" or possessions of these new colonists. Abraham had carried down 318 fighting men; Jacob may easily have had 1,500. Joseph made his brothers chief herdsmen of the royal flocks. Soon after, the crown owned all the land,

and then there was fertile pasturage in the Fayoum. In the first numbering, Moses showed 603,550 soldiers; twenty years after, near Jericho, 601,730. There had been losses by war, sickness, hardship, and discipline. Their bondage could not have begun till the Shepherds, a protecting kindred race, were driven out of the city of Avaris (the Scriptural Raamses), in the Delta, in the tenth year of Tuthmosis III. This oppressor was so hated, that cowardly, fanatical Menepthah could never complete his tomb. In this year he began his great building operations; 215 years from this, the Scripture period brings us to 1320 B.C., our assumed year of the Exodus! The king, who knew not Joseph, was a Pharaoh from the lately reconquered Upper Egypt. Sesortosen I. is the Sesostris of Herodotus. Birch gives us a remarkable inscription from the tomb of a lieutenant of his army, which says, in the person of the dead man, "When, in the time of Sesortosen I., there was a great famine in all the districts, there was corn in mine."

Only a sovereign, firm in power, could have lifted a hated slave into a viceroy. The position is changed again before Joseph asks permission to carry the body of Jacob into Hebron. He is then a rich man, but a private citizen; and makes his request humbly, through a servant. Reckoning back from this period — the period of the famine — will help us to adjust the earlier chronology. The Scripture seems to imply that Abraham lived 175 years; Isaac, 180; Jacob, 147; and Joseph, 110. Now we have historical records far older than the time of Abraham, but we know of no historical lives succeeding each other like these. These must be *eras of migration*, then, as Bunsen thinks; a supposition strengthened by the recently discovered fact, that the Jews of Cochin China continue to date *after the Exodus*.

Abraham emigrated into Canaan 2877 B.C. Isaac, born in the 26th year after this emigration, died in the 100th year *of Abraham*, aged 80. Jacob died in the 147th year of this era, or 42 years after his father. The Egyptian Hebrews, however, began a new era with the period of Jacob's coming into that country, and Joseph died in the 110th *year of Jacob*. Jacob was 70 when he went down into Egypt, in the 130th year of Abraham, and he lived to be 98. Joseph died at 78, in the 110th year of Jacob, when his great-grandson was 12 years old.

At the time of Abraham's migration, the whole of Canaan and East Jordan was tributary to the king of Elam. This included South Babylonia, Arabia Petræa, and the plain. The allied kings of the five cities were therefore a small body, and Abraham pursued only one detachment of their forces. Oldest inscriptions tell us that civilization came from South Babylonia. Rawlinson identifies "Kedorlaomer" with the "Kedor-mapula," or conqueror of the West, in these inscriptions. The circumstances by which Abraham was surrounded can be found at no later date than we assign to him. This is confirmed by the astronomically ascertained date of the destruction of the cities of the plain, which occurred about the time of Isaac's birth in 2854 B.C. Justin, borrowing from Trogus Pompeius, says, "The *ancestors of the Phœnicians* were compelled, by an earthquake near the Assyrian lake, to seek the coast." Now the chronology of Melkarth, in the island of Tyre, began in 2750 B.C. There was in Tyre a still older shrine, so they may easily have come to the coast a century earlier.

THE BONDAGE.

If the Israelites went into Egypt in the ninth year of Sesortosen I., 2754 B.C., and stayed there till the eleventh of Menepthah, 1320 B.C., they were there 1,434 years (according to computations of Bunsen's first four volumes). In this period they changed from a nomadic to an agricultural people, and it closed with 215 years of bondage. In the first 200 years, if not beloved, they prospered greatly, and spread throughout the country as itinerant traders. When the Hyksos came in, their knowledge of the country might easily be valuable to these new rulers of a kindred race. The power of the Hyksos lasted for 929 years. From the restoration under Amos to the oppression of Tuthmosis III., they doubtless kept very quiet; but union, independence, and national character were stimulated by 215 years of endurance. The building of the canal opened a hope of escape; then came Moses, the secret arming, and the Exodus. Fourteen hundred years is not too long for a people to grow from one family to two millions and a half of souls. It is perfectly clear that a period of this length is required to make the life of Abraham the legend Moses found it. The ancestors of Abraham are before chronology. Yet there is a strict chronology of the South-Babylonian empire, nearly a thousand years older; *i.e.*, back to 3758 B.C. Abraham undoubtedly possessed some memorials of the 2,000 years before his own time, — of the flood, &c. The traditions have a strict astronomical basis. The interval between Noah and Terah seems to proceed by similar *geographic* and *historic* methods. See Gen. x. 21.

From Apollonius Molon, it is said in Eusebius: "Man — *i.e.*, Edom or Adam — was driven, after the Flood, from Armenia to Syria. This took place three generations before Abraham. Abram had two sons; one was the father of twelve Arab princes. From the Laugher (Isaac) descended twelve sons, of whom the youngest, Joseph, was the ancestor of Moses."

Arphaxad is the district of Arrapakhitis, on the southwestern slope of the mountains, where the first men took refuge from flood and disaster on the northern plains. Elam is South Babylonia to the east of the Tigris; Assur is to the east of the Upper Tigris; Arphaxad, then, is near the sources of the Euphrates. Lud went to Asia Minor, crossed the Halys, and settled Lydia. The Aramœans or Highlanders passed from Arphaxad into the land of the "Two Rivers" (see Aram and Uz in Nedjir), as far as Northern Arabia.

These geographical periods passed, then come the purely historical, — "The Mission," or the advanced settlement; "The Partition," or the division of lands, as when Abraham and Lot separated later; "The Passage," or the crossing of the Tigris. In the "Mission," the race descended from the hills; in the "Partition," a part branched off to South Arabia; in the "Passage," they crossed the Upper Tigris to the south-west. Then come two geographical entries, — Rohi (the old name of Edessa), in Haran; and Serug, to the west of it, once Osröene; south-east were Resen and Ur of the Chaldees: places fixed, by the genius of D'Anville, before Niebuhr found them. The names of Nahor and Terah are the first names of persons.

Here we give the table which expresses the facts: —

Elam or S. Babylon.	*Assur* or Assyria.	*Arphaxad.* Primitive Chaldea, toward Assyria. 438 years.	*Lud.* Lydia on the Halys.	*Aram* or Syria.
		The Mission. Selah, 432 years.	*Uz in* N. Arabia.	*Hul. Geta,* Mts. near Lebanon.
		Heber. The Passage of the Tigris. 464 years.		
		Peleg. The Partition, 239 years.	*S. Arabia.* Toytan, father of 13 tribes.	
		Rohi, Edessa. Shepherds. 239 years.		
		Serug, Osröene. 230 years.		
		Nahor to Ur. 148 years from the Skirtus.		
		Terah to Haran. 275 years from Ur.		

10

Or, 70+205, — his age added to the year dated from his emigration, an accident which seems to have happened more than once. The 148 years of Nahor are from the date of the settlement on the Skirtus, near Ur and Haran. Terah begat three sons at the age of seventy. Sons born to previous generations were born at a natural period. The chronology of Ur began with Nahor; and these children were probably born in the 70th year of that chronology. Terah then moves from Ur to Haran, with Abram, aged 45; and Abram's wife, and Lot his grandson, in the 70th year of Ur. Five years after, at the age of 50, Abram moves on to Canaan, where Terah had intended to go. Now add to the 148 years from the Skirtus the 70 of Ur, and we have 218 years. Terah was thirteen at the time of his emigration, which, taken away, leaves 205. Therefore, —

From Arphaxad to Nahor are 933 years.
to death of Terah, 70 ,,
to Abram in Canaan, 5 years. = 1,008 years.

Which brings the post-diluvian origines to 3885 or 4000 B.C. The chronology of Egypt is fixed as far back as 3623 B.C.; that of Babylon to 3784 B.C. These last dates certainly represent a civilization which it had taken thousands of years to form.

Having indicated, in the outlines of the Egyptian dynasties, the date of the Exodus, we have travelled backward from it to the period of the original distribution of races, along the Scripture record. It is impossible to give here the demonstrations which have filled nearly five thousand octavo pages; but we see nothing careless, nothing purely speculative, in Bunsen's work. We now return to the Exodus, and work out the descending historic line.

THE EXODUS.

After the death of Raamses II., the oppressor of the nineteenth dynasty, Egypt fell into decay. His reign had produced every symptom of revolt. The Shepherds made frequent inroads. To clear the country, Menepthah sent all the kindred "lepers" into the quarries on the edge of Arabia. At last, he allowed them, or the chances of civil disturbance allowed them, to gather in the old city of the Hebrews, — Avaris, or Raamses. There they prepared for an outbreak. A priest of Heliopolis there founded a religious brotherhood, in direct opposition to the religion of the country. Menepthah went out against them, but the courage of the cowardly fanatic failed at the last. He left his captains to follow through the sea, and fled with the gods he ignorantly worshipped. He took with him to Ethiopia his son, Sethos II., then five years old. For thirteen years, the Shepherds desolated Egypt. Either this is the Egyptian account of the Exodus, or their records say nothing about it. In this account, Moses is called Oarsiph, "beloved of Osiris;" as if the gods of Egypt had once approved of him. The Shepherds were his allies.

ARGUMENTS.

1. It was not until the Shepherds were driven back, in the time of Tuthmosis III., that the Pharaohs would have dared to ill-treat the Hebrews. Sethos I. and Raamses II. were the oppressors; and, afterward, the religious fanaticism of Menepthah made the Jews desperate. It is quite clear, that Moses could not have conferred with Aaron, and armed his men, at a time when Egypt ruled the peninsula.

2. The Jews were certainly not *in* Palestine at any time previous to this: for the great Raamses conquered Palestine; and all its people and tribes, afterwards driven out by

the Jews, are enumerated on the monuments of his conquests. The names of Hittites and Amorites we find, but not the name of the children of Israel.

3. The "Solymites," or Shepherds, were expelled by Sethos II.; and when Josephus says, that the Hebrews went out through Sinai, in the reign of *Bocchoris*, he does not speak of another sovereign, but merely gives the official or "throne name" of Menepthah. Raamses had been strong; Menepthah was weak. The store-city the Hebrews had been compelled to build was called after their oppressor. In his records occurs the name Tanet-r, or *Holy Land*, by which the *Phœnicians* had designated their country from the beginning. In a papyrus-roll of his reign, preserved at Leyden, the scribe Kanitsir writes to his chief: "Now, I have heard the message which my Lord sent, saying, Give corn to the men and soldiers and Hebrews, who are drawing the stone for the great fortress of the palace of Raamses, lover of Truth, delivered to the general, Amennema. I have given them their corn every month, according to the good instruction of my Lord." The original of this paper is given in Bunsen's fifth volume. One of the objects in building these gigantic cities, whose separate structures are enumerated in the papyrus of Pinebsa, now in the British Museum, is indicated by a treaty, recorded on the walls of Thebes, between Raamses II. and Chetasar, King of the Hittites: "If the subjects of Raamses go over to Chetasar, that king is to compel them to return."

At the time that Moses was born and educated, whatever may have been the condition of the government, the civilization and literature of the Egyptians had reached their highest point. How ancient royal libraries were, we have no means of telling. The earliest papyri represent scribes registering flocks and harvests. In the first recorded dynasty, they had already "Annals of the Monarchy." The

"Annals of the New Empire" extended fifteen hundred years farther back than any ancient records known. A fragment of Livy, at Berlin, dated in the first century of our era, is the oldest manuscript out of Egypt. The "Book of the Dead," at Turin, goes back to the thirteenth century B.C. Songs, annals, almanacs, and contracts were frequently packed into the vases in the tombs. Raamses, the oppressor, built a library at Thebes, 1350 B.C., — thirty years before the Exodus. Its ruins, as described by Diodorus (i. 49), may still be traced; and at the entrance sat Thoth and Saf, the gods of Wisdom and History. Behind Wisdom, with significant transcendentalism, sat the god of *Hearing;* behind History, the god of *Seeing.* Many existing papyri were written in this Rameseion. Lepsius found at Thebes the tombs of the librarians. The office of Neb-nufre, "Superior over the books," was hereditary. This was not the first library; for, long before the gods of Wisdom and History had for titles the " Master and Mistress of the Hall of Books." — "They, of all people, stored up most for recollection," said Herodotus; so a library of 400,000 volumes was easily collected in Alexandria, at a time when the private collection of Aristotle served for all Greece. There Thales learned to measure heights by shadows; there Archimedes perfected his water-screw, and Eudoxus built his observatory. Shall we ever know what modern civilization owes to Egypt? Thence came the numerals; thence, thinks Taylor, all modern weights and measures. We never suspect, when we fill our demijohn, that it is the very vessel Moses called a "damagan."

It was in Egypt that Pythagoras first heard of immortality. The records show that the priests believed in one God. *They* held the name of God unpronounceable, and expressed him by the Hebrew formula, "I am that I am," — "*nuk-pu-nuk.*" It is a curious question, that no one seems able to answer, whether this formula is found in priestly records before the era when Moses himself might have given the impulse to such a faith.

We have shown that the era of the Exodus can be precisely fixed, by ascertaining the year in which the 15th of Epiphi corresponded to the April full-moon. It is impossible that there should be any doubt extending over fifty or sixty years since the Sothiac cycle began in Menepthah's reign, — a point as clearly fixed as our own leap-year.

JEWISH CHRONOLOGY, THEN, HAS THREE PERIODS: —

1. The period of Exodus, closing eighteen years after the death of Moses.
2. The time of the Judges, and the undivided kingdom.
3. The period of the kings of the divided kingdom.

1. EXODUS.

Year of Exodus.	B.C.
1. The 15th of Epiphi, the Exodus took place	1320
2. The Jews leave Sinai, in the second month	1319
3. Miriam dies in the first month	1318

They journey from Kadesh to Akaba, with one month's rest at Hor. The middle of this year, they arrive at the brook Zend, the south-eastern part of the Red Sea.

4. ⎫	1317
5. ⎬ They advance to the North, over against Jericho.	1316
6. ⎭	1315
22. The end of Moses' leadership occurs	1299
23. The first year of Joshua comes	1298
36. The last year of Raamses in Canaan	1287
40. The last year of Joshua east of Jordan is	1281
41. Joshua crosses Jordan six years after Raamses, or	1280
42 to 46. Joshua's six years of war in Canaan bring us to	1275
47. The death of Joshua, in the 47th year of the Exodus to	1274

Eighteen years intervene before they pay tribute to Mesopotamia; three hundred, before the building of the temple, 1014 B.C., — a date astronomically and critically determined.

Moses went into Midian in the life of Raamses II. He returned to find Menepthah on the throne. In the nineteenth year after the death of Joshua, the Jews became tributary to the Assyrians. They remained so until the election of Saul. The first "Shepherds" of the *Fifteenth Dynasty* were Arabs, whose names correspond to the Amalekite rule, which, the Arabs say, lasted eight hundred years in Egypt. The second were, doubtless, Southern Palestinians akin to Jethro. What created the mutiny at Kadesh Barnea, when the Jews desired so earnestly to return to Egypt? Only five days away, on the direct route of the caravans, where they could hear of the dismay of the Egyptians, of the successful inroads that followed the Exodus, they desired to return, and enrich themselves. This was the real difficulty Moses had to meet. He and Aaron threw themselves upon their faces to pray for aid, and finally led the Hebrews round the Gulf of Akaba, into the country east of Jordan. How great must have been the enthusiasm and faith that conquered!

The coincidences which determine these points are found in three separate lines of investigation, and cannot be accidental. Nor is there any satisfactory account to be given of the tributary condition of the Hebrews, nineteen years after the death of Joshua, except the sudden rise of the Assyrian power. The enumeration, in the twelfth chapter of Joshua, is a cotemporary document. This is proved by the account, in the first chapter, of their taking possession of Canaan; and the mention of Kirjath Sipher, or the "City of Writing," by its early name. The nations they had dispossessed now paid them tribute. The two tribes and a half beyond Jordan formed a living wall; yet, when they became tributary to Mesopotamia, 1246 B.C., they remained so for one hundred and seventy-five years. Nothing changed, but the names of their rulers. Under David, they rose, for the first time, to the height of power, which had enabled them to take possession of Canaan in the beginning. No imperfection of their own government will explain this continued dependence. That was due to the rising power of Assyria. Semiramis was no myth, but a Phœnician of the hated race they knew, — the wife of the Assyrian satrap at Ascalon.

POINTS SETTLED.

1. The Exodus can only have been possible between 1324 and 1320 B.C.
2. The undisturbed possession of the peninsula is only to be explained by the war in Egypt.
3. Moses determined the destiny of the Hebrews at Kadesh.
4. Canaan could not have been conquered seven years earlier than 1280 B.C., for Raamses was then raging through Palestine; nor seven years later, for Assyria then claimed it.
5. The original difficulties grow out of our possessing only a few shreds of the old story.

From the Exodus to the death of Joshua, then, was . 65 years.
The supremacy of Mesopotamia lasted . . . . . 8 ,,
The time of Othniel, Independence, and the Judges lasted . . . . 7 ,,
The supremacy of Moab . . . . 18 ,,
,, Ehud . . . . 7 ,,
,, N. Canaan . . . . 20 ,,
,, Barak and Deborah . . . . . 7 ,,
,, Midian . . . . — ,,
,, Gideon . . . . 17 ,,
,, Abimelech, son of Gideon . . . 3 ,,
Of Tola, Ibdam, Elon, and Abdon in Canaan . . . 48 ,,
Of Jair, the Ammonites, and Jepthah in E. Jordan . 48 ,,

SUPREMACY OF THE PHILISTINES.

The rule of the High Priests lasted . . . . 40 years.
Sixty-six years were divided by { Saul . . . . . 22 ,,
David . . . . . 41 ,,
Solomon . . . . 3 ,,
And the Jews lived in Disunion 306 years.

This whole period coincides with the Assyrian supremacy in Western Asia. It began the year after Joshua's death, 1273 B.C., and came to its height at the death of Semiramis, in 1222 B.C. Sardanapalus is the Tiglath Pileser of the Scripture; and, in his day, the Jews were carried to Babylon (see Judges iii. 8). Khusan Risathaim, the Judge of the Two Rivers, was the Assyrian satrap who had married Semiramis. In the Assyrian tongue, this name means only satrap of Mesopotamia. For Semiramis, Palestine was only a bridge to Egypt, which she conquered in 1250 B.C., twenty-three years later. Her successors strained every nerve to get possession of it.

There is no instance, known to us, of a history so faithful to *its own purpose* as that of our own Scripture.

The Old Empire of Egypt was isolated as that of China was. The New Empire was drawn under the influence and policy of Asia. That was a noble life, which the long Hyksos usurpation had chilled; and, if the New Empire had not expelled the Hebrews, it might have come to new power. To the Egyptians, therefore, the Exodus was God's judgment, — a link in a well-devised plan of avenging justice. A new invasion of Palestinians was merely a cover for the Exodus, — the Sicilian vespers in which Asia avenged herself on Egypt! When, in the third year of Menepthah, such invaders slew the first-born, they were messengers of the Most High, in Hebrew eyes. When the king fled, the invaders plundered all the Delta, and, to his fanatical horror, devoured all the sacred animals. Very likely, Jethro incited this invasion. It was the death-blow of the New Empire. In thirteen years, the invaders were expelled; but the strength of the nation was gone for ever. The *Nineteenth Dynasty* outlived the Exodus only twenty-two years. Raamses III., the "Man of Memphis," restored order. He conquered back the old renown, and erected sumptuous buildings. In the fiftieth year of this Dynasty, 1280 B.C.,

Semiramis conquered Egypt. No more victories, no more monuments. Shishak, the founder of the *Twenty-Second Dynasty*, ransacked Jerusalem in the reign of Rehoboam. The names of *his* family indicate some Assyrian connection. Two hundred and fifty years before, in the time of Eli, the high priest, Raamses XII., had sent a sacred mission from Thebes to Nineveh. Perhaps it went to cure of some illness Nefruari, "Beauty of the Sun," who is recorded to have been healed, and married to Raamses. This account, given by Macrobius and a stele in the Louvre, translated by Champollion, may indicate the opening of an alliance, which ended by breaking up the isolation of the empire. In the reign of David, an Edomite prince had taken refuge in Egypt. Solomon married Pharaoh's daughter. War-chariots and cavalry were sent to him from Egypt. Hezekiah evidently thought it bad policy to lean on Egypt; yet kindly memories prevailed with him over the memories of the bondage. "Thou shalt not abhor an Egyptian, for thou wert a stranger in his land," is said in Deut. xxiii. 7, 8, *et seq.* See also —

	B C.
Hosea xi. 16	770
Zechariah ix. 11	734
Nahum	733
Isaiah vii.	740

Rahab, which means a "blustering do-nothing," is used for the first time in Isa. xxx. 1-7.

	B.C.
Jeremiah xliii.–xliv.	604 to 585
Ezekiel xxix. 1-16	588

These Scripture references fill out the historic picture.

THE PENTATEUCH.

In some portions of this book, God is called "Elohim," with the verb in the singular. The word might be rendered as

an abstraction, "God-head." In others, he is designated as "Jahveh,"—pronounced Jăhovah, improperly, by throwing into it the vowels of the word Adonai (Lord), usually written beneath it, to show that it was unpronounceable; thus: J. H. V. H.
ă o a

Tuch shows that the Elohim is a connected story, to which the Jewish Jehovist, thinking to fill a gap, adds his scraps of tradition.

    1st. We have in it the earliest Registers, or Pedigrees.
    2d. Brief memóranda attached to them.
    3d. Songs commemorative of great events.
    4th. Detailed stories.

In Genesis, then, under the first head, we have to compare two entirely different registers.

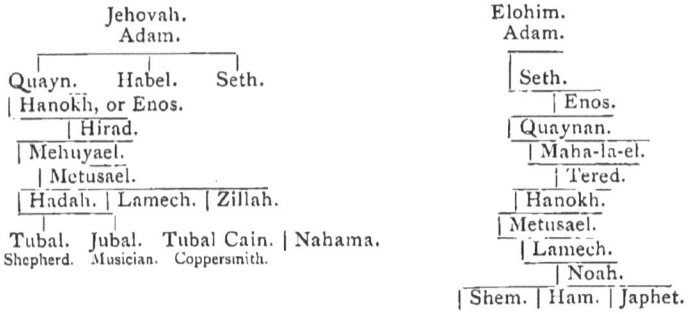

In the oldest record, God is called Jahveh Elohim. This is the story from Aramea. In the later, he is called Seth, or Set; and man is called Enos. This is the tradition of Phœnicia. The Aramean tradition does not come down to the time of the flood, or rather has no necessity to deal with it, since it does not follow the descendants of Lamech. The other includes it, and tells of the house of Noah. At Iconium, in Asia Minor, Hanokh, the father of Lamech, is said to have predicted the flood, but no one would listen. Of the three races, —

Ham or Cham = Chem, means the *dark*.
Sem, the *glowing;* from whom came Adam or Edom the *red*, whence Phœnician, also the *red*.
Japhet was the *fair*.

Of purely mythical names, we have, in the Bible accounts, Set, Enos, Adam, Havvah, the Life-Giving, and Abel, the Vanishing. Quain is the type of those who bear arms, and cultivate the soil.

Nod is flight.
Cain, Nad, or the fugitive..
Hanokh means " taught of God."

A life of three hundred and sixty-five years seems to indicate a mythical character: —

Hirad means " citizen."
Ma-hu-ya-el, " struck of God."
Metusael, " Man of God."
Lamech, the " Robber."
Hadah, " Beauty."
Zillah, a " Shadow."

The man of God stands between Cain, the Marauder, and Ired, "Builder of cities."

CONCLUSIONS.

I. The orders of Gods, Semitic, Egyptian, and Greek, are identical.

II. They belong to primeval conceptions.

III. The Biblical story is the only one free from great monstrosity.

IV. In that is the Ideal element of one God, restored by Abraham. The historic element consists of primitive Aramaic recollections.

V. The historic record does not, at first, refer to men; but to certain epochs, or changes of residence, of which the record had descended, but was not understood.

RESTORATION OF REGISTER.

God as Jehovah Elohim,	God as Seth, or Seti.
created.	
Adam the Red, or	Enos the Strong.
Humanity develops as	
I. Cain the Smith, before whom the nomad disappears; also, a builder of cities.	I. Cain, or Quayn, &c.
II. Hanokh, the Seer and the God of the solar year.	IV. Hanokh.
III. Hirad, dweller in towns.	III. Ired.
IV. Ma-hu-ya-el, " God-struck."	II. Ma-ha-la-el.
V. Metusael, man of God.	V. Metusael.
VI. Lamech, the Strong.	VI. Lamech.

The key to this restoration was given us by the Mosaic author, when he put the two registers in juxtaposition.

Till the time of Joel, there was no tampering with this record. First came changes in the Samaritan, then in the Septuagint; then Eusebius altered it to produce ecclesiastical conformity. Then came the two monks, — the Byzantines, Amianas and Panodorus, — with their schemes of reduction.

AN APPROXIMATION TO EPOCHS ON BUNSEN'S PLAN.

The rule of Seth = 912 years; that of Adam = 930 years; that of Enos = 905 years. Of course, these periods are set aside as mythical. Seth is a God; Adam and Enos equally represent the first man.

SECOND EPOCH.

Kenaan lived	910 years.
Mahalael „	895 „
Ired „	962 „
Hanokh „	365 „
Metusael „	967 „
Lamech „	777 „ = 4,878 years in all.

EPOCH OF THE FLOOD.

Noah lived 600 hundred years before the flood. This is the great cosmic period of the Patriarchs, the equation of the solar and lunar years. Josephus tells us of it. Fréret has unravelled it. Make the calculation, and we shall see that the previous epochs of the primeval world were supposed to have lasted eight cycles.

Then Noah's life to the flood was 600 years, or the 9th cycle.
Shem's = 600 ,, ,, 10th cycle.

Of the 350 years Noah is said to have lived *after* the flood, fifty belong to the period before the flood, where the astronomical calculation is deficient to just that extent.* We see, therefore, that all *estimates of time*, before the removal of the race to Arphaxad, were *cyclical*. We must now try to discover how the geographical dates which marked the descent from the mountains, changed into eras marked by the life or names of individuals.

The years of Noah after the flood were half a cycle . 300 years.
The years of Shem were a cycle . . . . 600 ,,
And cyclical time after the flood was . . . . . . 900 ,,

HISTORICAL AND GEOGRAPHICAL PERIODS.

The residence in Arphaxad was . . . 438 years.
In Selah, the Mission . . . . 433 ,,
,, Heber, the Crossing . . . . . . 464 ,,
,, Peleg, the Partition . . . . . . 239 ,,
,, Rehu, the Pastoral . . . . . . 239 ,,
,, Serug or Osroene . . . . 230 ,,
,, Nahor, colonies in Padan Aram . . 148 ,,
,, Terah in Haran, Abram till 75 years old 275 years = 2,466 years.

---

* I have not been able to find the explanation of this assumption. It may be in some inedited paper of Fréret.

The distinctly historic period begins with Arrapakhitis. In round numbers, this dates back to 5000 B.C. In Selah, the settlements were pushed forward. In Heber, they crossed the Tigris; and then all the advances are to the Southwest, till Abraham crosses the Euphrates. Terah is, perhaps, a person merged in an epoch. He not only went *to Haran*, it will be seen, but his *son Haran* died before he went. Did he name the new land for the dead son? It is evident the record was made when the name had become fixed. After the cyclical period, we have another, evidently indefinable, before the Semites dispersed in the highlands of Asia. Now the history of Chamitic life in Egypt requires 4,000 years before the Aramaic emigration. During this primitive time, can we find any space for the story of Nimrod and Babel? This is either a myth, or the oldest fragment of history in the world. Now, Nimrod, the Kossack (not Cushite, but Koshite), could not have lived later than 4000 B.C. The Kossians were an ancient Scythian tribe in the mountains, east of the Tigris. These people, a far older race than the Semitic, lived in the plains of Shinar. It would seem as if the marauding life of Nimrod might have driven them across the Tigris, and started the emigration that followed. If we make the first historical starting-point, Babylon, 3784 B.C., we leave room for Nimrod. His was not a transient influence: it was as subversive and permanent as the fancied confounding of speech, which followed the destruction of his tower. It is to this day deeply impressed upon the Asiatic continent.

Philo of Byblus said, "Babylon was not built by Semiramis, as Herodotus said; but by Babylon, son of Belus, 2,000 years before." Before the building of Babylon, there was a long line of forgotten Chaldean kings, and in their history that of Nimrod forms the first decisive break. He, the Kossack, invaded their territory, and built in their field a mighty watch-tower. *Their* descendants overthrew *his* usurped dominion before the building of the city. The consequences of the mixing and scattering of races which ensued, were momentous, and tradition preserved them. The first compiler of the record knew nothing of the Koshite tribe, and misunderstood the reference.

ABRAHAM.

Abraham did not hesitate to adopt or fall into the Phœnician dialect, although he rejected the Phœnician faith. If *he* preserved his native Aramaic, a mixed family of dependents could not be expected to do so. The old tongue of Tyre and Sidon is pure Hebrew. If he had turned with horror from the idolatry of Aram, that of Phœnicia was far more corrupt; but in spite of him, and very naturally, many mythological references were mixed up with the narrative of his descendants.

Evangelical Christians say that Jesus was crucified on Freya's day, or Friday, and see no impropriety in it. The mixed use of Elohim, Jehovah, and Seth, in the narrative, shows that the old Hebrews fell into similar habits. The patriarchs were historical persons; but, between Joseph and Moses, many symbols and stories of the pre-Abramic period got interwoven with the popular Epos. The names of Esau and Israel were mythological, borrowed from Phœnician story, perhaps indignantly applied in retort for claims set up for these false gods. Thus, the name of Is-ra-El may have been the proud assertion that their chief was the true and only "Wrestler with God."

We have already sketched the Egyptian framework into which the Hebrew narrative should be fitted. We then proceeded to fix the period of the Exodus, and worked backward and forward from it till we had outlined the Hebrew story subsequent to Abraham. Then we went back to the Pentateuch, and dissected its registers; a work which would have been unintelligible in the beginning, and if undertaken without the light shed on it by the later story. The reader who would profit from what is set before him, must consent to work. Bunsen's pages will never serve to wile away an idle moment.

Having left the Hebrew branch of our great inquiry in a form likely to be interesting and useful to the Biblical student, we proceed to mention some matters purely critical, and to touch upon some others relating to the literature and mythologies of Phœnicia and Egypt, and necessary to the student who would inquire further. Since the Armenian version of Eusebius, the authority of Berosus is undisputed. We may expect still to excavate from Phœnicia some remains of the time of Abraham. The burial of Jacob at Hebron seems attested by the immense ruins there; and whatever shakes the basis of Ottoman power in the Holy Land, will make it possible to investigate that site. While Bunsen was writing, the sarcophagus of Ashmuneser, king of Sidon, was discovered, and carried to France. Why could not the walls of the Louvre charm away its secret? Then, perhaps, it could have told us whether Homer was blind, whether Semiramis sent to Sidon for its famous glass mirrors, and who bought the Palais-Royal jewelry manufactured there in the Trojan era! Bunsen does not doubt that Philo of Byblus had access to very important records; that the San-Con-Iath was not so much the work of one author, as the earliest sacred book of Phœnicia preserved like the Torah of the Jews. Long before the time of Hiram, they must have had permanent records; and that king introduced many changes into the sacred calendar. Access to such records explains why Philo tacked together two different cosmogonies, like the old writer in Genesis, and the fragments he preserves of the San-Con-Iath are a brilliant confirmation of the historical character of the Bible tradition.

As regards the origin of the Semitic name for God (Sun, Fire), there is no doubt that I A O, the Phœnician name, is the abbreviation of IABE or IEHOVAH. Urim and Thummin, Phœnician Light and Truth, beamed from the Hebrew priests' breast-plate. The Kerubim (cherubim) of the garden were only revolving flames, the tradition of which kept the emigrants from turning back; perhaps because a volcanic agency preceded the overwhelming flood. Seraphim meant, in the beginning, running flames, from which it came to be applied to poisonous snakes. The old form of El gave the four eyes to the Kerubim, and the six wings to the Seraphim. Yet the recent title of an article, "The God of Israel *once* the Sun god," does not convey the truth. The nations of Central Asia were the worshippers of an invisible God, like the North-American Indians; and it was to that original faith that Abraham returned when surrounding idolatries had corrupted the customs of his people. The oldest authentic name of God is Seth. Set-Typhon corresponds to Saturn. The sacred Dog-Star, Sothis, bears the same name. In the Bible, Seth is the father of Enos or Man. Kevan is the name translated Chiun or Keeun (Amos v. 26), which was the idol worshipped in the wilderness.

A few points of contact between the Biblical and the Phœnician stories deserve attention. Hercules wrestled with "Typhon," "the meridian sun in the sand," as Jacob wrestled with El-ohim. He was wounded, like Jacob, in the thigh; and, like him, called the Wrestler (Isra = Palaimon). Usov, his brother, was a hunter who wore shaggy skins, and, like the Hebrew Esau, went away from home to live. The great pair of Gods were El-iun and Behuth, Adoni and Baalti, Lord and Mistress. The God El sacrifices Yadid, his "only-begotten" and "well-beloved son," and beheads his daughter Zillah. If the God would sacrifice his children, of course the man must, or obversely; if the man did, the God must: and at last the prostitution of womanhood, and the sacrifice of manhood, symbolized by circumcision, were substituted for death.

Tauthe or Thoth, is said to have invented the first alphabet, made of serpents. Canaan had a brother who added to this Phœnician alphabet three letters. He was called Aram; he was the Syrios of Herodotus: and Bunsen believes that it was Abraham the Syrian who thus completed the alphabet. What relation serpents had to the *earliest alphabet*, it is now impossible to say. Philo says that the Greek Theta owed its form to the Egyptian habit of designating the Deity by a ringed serpent, with its head turned inward, the dot representing the eye of God in the world. But the serpent was the name and symbol of the Phœnician letter Tet, which preceded the Greek Theta; and that Greek letter *still represents the Deity* in abbreviated writing. When knowledge was considered a Divine thing, forbidden to the mass of men, it is not wonderful that letters should grow out of cabalistic signs.

The psychical myth was represented by Osiris. His worship is the intellectual centre of the worship of Egypt. The perfect soul is the son of God, Osiris; Man, who, having passed through the judgments of the lower world, was at last reconciled to his Father.

NOTATIONS OF RELIGIOUS DEVELOPMENT.

I. Cosmogonic worship, as of Ptah, or Hephaistos.
II. Of the Solar Power, as in Ra, or Helios.
III. Of Time and Space, as Seb and Nu.
IV. Of Psychical worship or the Divine Rule of Man, as in Osiris.

Ptah is the oldest God, as yet unendowed with the symbols of the Sun. He is an Ideal. Only a Creator. He is the God who shapes the Cosmic egg on the potter's wheel. Helios and his successors represent the solar power, and bear its symbols. In Osiris, God himself appears as man, the child of Time and Space,—a myth which has not yet lost rule over the minds of men. Upper Egypt calls this divine man Osiris. Lower Egypt calls him Seth. Seth is the Phallic-god, type of the sun, in the rage of the Dog-Star. Osiris is not a deified man, but justified man is God as Osiris. The story of Osiris is the story of the circle of the year, of the sun dying away and resuscitating itself again. His name is a riddle. Isis is its first element. It is written Hes-Iri. This means "eye of the world;" but it is probable that a better meaning attached to it, as a primitive Aramaic root.

HS. is the name and sign of the Throne of Isis. H. S toreth, or throne of Astarte, indicates this also; but how came the Egyptians to use only the first syllable of this name, and what does it mean? Philo says that Astarte found a star which had dropped from Heaven. She picked it up, and put it in the temple at Tyre. Now the polar star of the Phœnicians was the brilliant Beta of the Little Bear, which the Arabs still call "The Star."

Three thousand years before Christ, this was nearer to the pole than any other conspicuous star. The above story merely tells us that it was sacred to Astarte. The Arabs call the square in the Great and Little Bears, the *Bier*, or N. HaS. Therefore it is evident that the worship of Astarte was coincident with the period when this star became the Pole-Star. It is not an Aramaic name; it is the word translated Arcturus in Job ix. 9, and xxxviii. 32. The Edomite colonies, driven by the convulsions of the Dead Sea to the coast, date from 2800 B.C., which coincides with the suggestions of the above statement. "Hes" has no meaning in the Egyptian. Hathor, however, meant the "world." The two "Has toreth" were thrown into one about 2000 B.C. HaS meant a bier; but HS., the accented form, meant "throne" or seat: the whole word, Hes-Asar, expressed the abstract conception of the Divine Power, — "Throne of the World." Hesiri is a rebus. Now the date of 2500 B.C. is given as the earliest at which this Beta of the Little Bear was likely to be used as a pole-star. The Chaldee system of astral symbols has its date determined in a similar way. The Bull (Tor) indicated the vernal equinox and generative power. This became possible in its actual astral connection 3000 B.C.

Here is a *Harmony of Names*, which shows whence Egypt *derived* language and religion; not indeed from Phœnicia, but from an older common source.

PHŒNICIAN.	EGYPTIAN.
Set,	Set.
Ba'al,	Bal.
(Ptah) the opener with seven forces, the Semitic week,	Pth. Hephaistos.
Esmun,	Esmun. Eighth Hermes.
Tet, the Serpent,	Tet. Hermes.
Amon, the Sculptor,	Amun, the concealed.
Nebo,	A-nebu.
Kon Heracles,	Khonsa. Heracles.
Ur, God of Light,	Her. God of Day.
Asar, the Mighty,	Hes-Iri-Hesar.
Hanokhe,	Anuke.
Teneth, Tenait,	N.T. Athena-Tenait.
HaS. (toreth) Throne,	HS. Throne.

Yet Renan denies that there is any philological connection between the Phœnician and the Egyptian. The studies of George Rawlinson, Master of Ancient History at Oxford, however, sustain Bunsen, even when Rawlinson is not aware of it himself. Ancient Cushite (Kossite) tribes coursed over the central Asiatic plains; and he shows that the ancient sacred Chaldean tongue was the Galla of Ethiopia, — the Biblical *Cush!* Set was an Egyptian Moloch. Egypt soon abolished human sacrifice. Osiris, who suffers like

Christ, ruled it with a law of conscience. The Egyptians were the first who made a dogma of the immortality of the soul. (See the "Book of the Dead," and the assertions of the Greeks confirmed by the monuments.) The belief in the transmigration of souls was a provincialism of their own. It was because of it that the Ethiopian animal worship at last conquered Egypt; or had that provincial belief been the first evidence of the Ethiopian influence? The "Book of the Dead" exhibits, as the groundwork of their religion, moral responsibility, of which we find few traces in the Vedas. There is a great similarity between their ideas of duty and those of the Decalogue, or the seven commands of Abraham, supposed to be so much older. The immortal soul is banished from God by misconduct. Faith charges the body with all sin, and would annihilate it; but Man shall see God at the end of his wanderings.

In the Egyptian novel of "The Two Brothers," the belief in transmigration furnishes the machinery. The hero may die as many times as the author pleases. He may become a tree; but at last his sin will be overtaken, and he will become a man. The builders of the Pyramids must save their bodies, if they would remain immortal; thus their fear of a people's indignation indirectly caused the erection of their monuments and the preservation of their records. Their literature consisted of religious books, hymns, prayers, and incantations and novels. Its wider scientific scope may be discovered by studying the character of the forty-two books of Hermes, as described by Clemens. Fragments of these books are gradually coming to the light. To one class of them — the "Ceremonial Books of the Stolists" — belongs the "Book of the Dead." From its pages we quote a few significant sentences: —

"I am the one who knows," says the Departed.
"The Osiris justified in peace is the Sun himself."
"I went in as a hawk, and came out as a Phœnix."

And this sentence, which might well be graven over the entrance of the Museum at Cambridge, and which it would be well for Owen and Darwin to consider as they write:—

"The Sem-sem, or genesis of a type, is the *greatest of secrets!*"

"Mashallah," a stele dated 4,000 B.C., and translated by Chabas for the "Archæological Review," of April 15, 1858, contains these sentences:—

"Having the courage which knowledge gives thee, converse with the ignorant as well as the learned. Is any master quite perfect?"

"If it humble thee to serve a wise man, thy conduct suits thy own relation to God. *He* knows thou art among *the little ones!* Do not make thy heart proud against him."

"The interior of a man is no secret to him who made it. He is with thee, though thou be alone."

The plot of "The Two Brothers," of which we have spoken in a theological connection, is genuine. It indicates the moral government of the world, and is illustrated by satirical drawings. In these, the world appears upside down: mice are eating cats; women are seizing men; and here, if not in the common heart and wit of man, the authors of the Batrachomyomachia and the Ecclesiazousæ might have found inspiration! The *sacred art* of Egypt was conventional, but its artist possessed skill of a very different kind. All the portraits in the great work of Lepsius indicate individuality and character. Tuthmosis II. has an unmeaning face; his sister's (whose escutcheons he erased) is commanding. Tuthmosis, the oppressor, is handsome. Horus looks like the weak enthusiast he was. The Asiatic profile of Raamses II. is well known; and his great father, Sethos I., has a still nobler face. Statues of private persons confirm this impression. A squatting, attentive figure of a scribe, now in the Louvre, is especially remarkable. Of the science and learning of the Egyptians, we have indicated enough in the course of this article. The time has not yet come when we dare to provoke the incredulity of our readers, by talking about steam-engines and telescopes. Lepsius found the roll of papyrus on the monuments of the Old Empire, and an inkstand is carried by a scribe of the Fourth Dynasty. Before Joseph was, Egypt had records and a literature!

In a recent lecture on Immortality, Emerson quoted the following words from Van Helmont: "It is my greatest desire that it might be granted unto atheists to have tasted at least, but only one moment, what it is *intellectually* to *understand*, whereby they may *feel* the immortality of the mind, as it were, *by touching;*" and he then went on to say substantially, "The man of courage is he who has tested his parts, knows how they will serve him, what uses they will endure, and of what fibre they are made; so he who deals with eternal things feels himself eternal." This feeling Bunsen confers upon all those who study him faithfully. He tests his own immortal powers constantly, and makes us conscious of our own.

It has been said that "Egypt's Place in History" is the "worst written book in the world." A book that undertakes to create a history, by working out an untold number of problems, — whose significance can only be felt, whose true sequence can only be perceived, by an advanced student, — may lay its author open to such a charge; but no one ever did justice to these books without "being lifted upon unseen wings," as Fredrika Bremer used to say; without being kindled by a glow of enthusiasm, drawing nearer to God, and taking hold more consciously of the soul's destiny. So to be uplifted and stimulated is to "deal with eternal things." There is a peculiar fitness in bringing the work of Bunsen adequately before the public at this moment. It is not only that the progress of years has justified him, in many positions which challenged at first the ridicule of the world; but the publication of his fifth volume offers to every student an opportunity to investigate the questions, which have sustained an irreparable loss, as it would seem, by the recent death of Dr. Boeckh at Berlin, and Dr. Hincks at London. To a clear statement of his Problems and their key, Bunsen here adds a Dictionary and Grammar of hieroglyphics, and a complete translation of the "Book of the Dead," of which there are several copies, and one, we hope, still in this country.

To this are added interesting Egyptian texts, with interlinear translations, on which the student may try the merits of the Grammar and Dictionary; and, still farther, a "Complete Comparison of the hitherto known Egyptian Words, both Old and New, with the Semitic." With such helps, we hope for a generation of Egyptian scholars in this country. We especially welcome the Appendix, because it clearly shows the justification of Bunsen's work. True, the name of the Holy Mykerrinus was long a myth, and to-day his coffin may be handled in the British Museum! True that men sneered at Bunsen, when he demanded an antiquity of 3,300 years for the reign of Cheops; and, lately, the independent labors of a Mussulman astronomer claim that the pyramid of Cheops must have been erected in the year 3285 B.C.!

Still, there are not wanting respectable scholars who produce Blair's magnificent tables of Chronology, and devoutly believe with him that the world was made Oct. 23, 4,004 years B.C. Bunsen's book is a wholesome rack for a cramped brain. In addition, then, to the great lists of kings, the palace registers, and tablets of the monuments, we welcome in this volume the new text of the age of Cheops, the Sallier papyrus detailing the quarrels of the Shepherds with the native rulers; the inscription at Tanis, which places 400 years between Raamses II. and the Hyksos rule; and the inscription at Karnak, recording an eclipse. The newly discovered tablet at San, containing the Greek translation of a decree, confirms the principles of hieroglyphic interpretation heretofore adopted. It bears witness to an immortal human intelligence, always competent to interpret transient human work. Here, too, are to be found the amended texts of Philo and others, who have interpreted the fragmentary traditions out of which the story has been in part woven. It is still necessary that a competent Editor should be found for these volumes, who will do in detail what we have attempted in general. The purpose of some of the tables is still obscure, and Dr. Birch only edits *the philology* of this last volume.

CAROLINE H. DALL.

BOSTON, *October 5th*, 1867.

SCHOLIA.

I ADD here, and under this title, a few facts, which I could not connect usefully with the text, and which may, nevertheless, answer some questions, to the more thoughtful students of this subject.

To these, I add my own synopses of the theories of John Taylor and Piazzi Smyth, because these men have thought it their duty to attack Baron Bunsen, in their mistaken devotion to the letter of the Scripture. Bunsen's measurements of the pyramids, derived from the authorities extant when he wrote, have seemed to me of so little importance, in connection with his theories, that I do not advert to them. Smyth, on the other hand, considers their necessary and inadvertent errors fit cause for doubting the soundness of all Bunsen's results. It is, therefore, well to look closely at Piazzi Smyth's own work ; and such of its results as are worth considering may be found in this Appendix.

I.

Carthage was founded 814 B.C. This is an important date for Bunsen. He gets through it a synchronism.

The fourth year of Solomon is the eleventh of Hiram, King of Tyre (2 Sam. v. 11 ; 1 Chron. iv. 1). Hiram sent cedar and workmen to David, and the same to Solomon. After the works were completed, Solomon gave Hiram twenty villages, and Hiram sent sailors to man Solomon's fleet. Hiram was, therefore, alive in the twenty-fourth year of Solomon ; therefore, the temple was built 1014 B.C.

	B.C.
Tyre was founded	1254
Ninus and Semiramis were on the throne	1273

Now, a papyrus of Raamses III. (1273 B.C.?) speaks of "Tyre as a city on the sea, which receives fishes from the water, and grain from the land," — a significant description, when we remember that the city was on the island as well as the main.

II.

	B.C.
Zoroaster's first year is	2234
Semiramis' first year	1273

The first year of Semiramis comes within six years after the last campaign of Raamses III., very soon after she conquered Egypt and Ethiopia. Egypt became tributary, and the tomb of Raamses was never finished. Semiramis took Cabul between 1235 and 1225 B.C. India had a king whose rule extended to the Indus at the time. Baghadatta must have been that king.

III.

The ancient Peruvians possessed charts, exhibiting the manner in which South America was peopled from Asia, through the islands of the Pacific. For a long time, these charts were regarded as clever impositions; but, since the recent discoveries of Speke and Baker have demonstrated the perfect correctness of the Arab charts of the thirteenth century, it behooves us to look well to all records and mementos on our own shore. If the photographs, brought to the Lowell Institute by Mr. Squier, prove any thing, it is the solstitial character of the Druidic circles at Abury and Stonehenge. The sacred inclosures of Peru, still called, in the native tongue, "the place where the sun is tied up," are identical in their structure; and we think it would be well to inquire before it is too late, whether there are not, among the unconverted tribes, definite traditions as to their use. The rush sails on Lake Titicaca, to-day, are managed in the same way as those carved into the walls of the sepulchre of Raamses III.

IV.

The Great Pyramid: Why was it Built? By JOHN TAYLOR. London: Longman, Green, & Longman, 1859; 2d edition, 1864.

This book has a certain interest in connection with the result of Bunsen's inquiry as to Egypt's place in history. Its main theory is, that the great pyramid at Ghizeh was built as a standard of mensuration, which standard was determined for the ancients by the diameter and circumference of the globe; the secret of its spherical shape having been already discovered. The azimuth of the entrance-passage coincides with the astronomical meridian of the place; and, that the standard of dry-measure might never be lost, the porphyry coffer of Cheops was built in to the sealed structure. Mr. Taylor proceeds to his statements, without the least regard to the inscriptions already deciphered in the pyramids themselves, and apparently ignorant that a building, erected in conformity to the ritual of an astral faith, would of necessity *preserve* such measures, whether erected for the purpose or not! Whatever we may think of the theory, the book is full of original suggestion, which the favorable mention of Herschel and Piazzi Smyth forbid the scholar to ignore. We proceed to extract the pith from his pages.

The early world bore traces of an antediluvian measure, in a certain sacred or double cubit, — the cubit of Karnak, estimated by Gardner Wilkinson, — and which Taylor finds to be the basis of every sort of mensuration in the Great Pyramid. A proof of the existence of the double cubit is preserved in Herodotus. The priests told him, that, in the reign of Moeris, the Nile overflowed all the land when it rose to the height of eight cubits; but, in the time of Herodotus, it had to rise to the height of *sixteen* cubits to overflow the same land. Eight cubits of Karnak, in use fifteen hundred years before Christ, were equal to sixteen cubits in use a thousand years later. Scripture is quoted (2 Chron. iii. 3) to show the use among the Hebrews of a double measure. The height of Solomon's temple, in 2 Chron. called a hundred and twenty, is represented in 1 Kings as equal to thirty cubits of the *first* measure. The fourth of the cubit of Karnak was a *span*. This cubit measure, derived from the earth's belt, may have had a relation to the mensuration of time. "There was signified on the pyramid," says Herodotus, by means of *Egyptian characters*, " how much was expended on radishes, onions, and garlic for the laborers; and, as I well remember, the interpreter, reading over, said it amounted to sixteen hundred talents of silver." Egyptian characters were generally pictorial, and Taylor believes the inscription to have been a measure of the earth's radius or diameter, indicated by the signs still in use, — as degrees (°), minutes ('), and seconds ('); these, cut in the stone, being not unlike vegetables. "The second of the diameter," he says, " is *sixteen inches*, of which measure there are three hundred and sixty in the 5,760 inches at present called a second."

" When the new earth was first measured after the Deluge [or Edenic convulsions, as Bunsen would say], it was found that it exceeded the diameter of the old earth by a distance equal to 36,868 miles." This change produced a change in all measures.

" The porphyry coffer, or " tomb of Cheops," — the pyramid having been built to preserve the sacred antediluvian measure, — is then considered. The coffer stands in the chamber, in the meridian, north and south, but only half the distance from the east wall that it is from the west. In this coffer we find the old measure of the chaldron (Latin, *caldarium*, or hot-bath), not used by us as a liquid measure, but naturally enough taking that name if measures were shaped like this coffer or the Hebrew laver, both precisely like a bath. He then shows the extraordinary coincidence of English measures with those of the coffer. Its contents are equal to 4 quarters of wheat = 128 pecks = 32 bushels = 4 Hebrew chomers = 128 Greek hecters = 128 Roman modii. Now a pint is equal to a pound; so, if our original chaldron were shaped like a trough (trö), from that would come Troy weight, or " trough weight," for solids.

> 24 barley-corns or 32 wheat-corns = 1 pennyweight.
> 20 pennyweights = 1 oz.
> 12 oz. = 1 lb.

There is no doubt, we suppose, that wheat originally determined all measures; but 8 lbs. of wheat Troy was equal in bulk to 10 lbs. of water, Troy weight. So any vessel that would hold 10 lbs. of water, only held 8 lbs. of corn. Before the phrase "Avoirdupois" came into use, the water-measure was expressed by the phrase " merchants' pound." All profits of sales were made by buying pounds of 16 ounces, to sell pounds of 12. The bakers' dozen of 13, sold out at 12, had a similar antiquity. The same base — *i.e.*, the cubit of Karnak — controlled the pyramid, Solomon's temple, the coffer of Cheops, and the chaldron of Henry III. The proportion of the diameter of a circle to its circumference is now represented by 1 to 3.1415927. When the pyramid was built, it was as 1 to 3.141792. This measure allows to the diameter 500 millions of inches, but these were *English inches!*

To the measures before the Flood, we owe the sacred cubit attributed to the Ark, — the Karnak cubit of the pyramid, and the primitive English mile of 5,760 feet, an eleventh part greater than the present mile. The coffer contains 256 gallons of water, each gallon weighing 10 lbs. merchants', or Avoirdupois, weight; also 256 gallons of wheat, each gallon weighing 10 lbs. Troy.

In England, by law, 32 grains of middle-sized wheat are equal to 24 grains Troy. He shows, in this connection, the origin of the English word *mud*, in the Mut or Μωτ of the San-Chun-Iath.

In commenting with interest on this book, Sir John Herschel says, "Mr. Taylor has the merit of pointing out, that the *same slope* belongs to any pyramid which has each of its faces superficially equal to the square described upon its height;" also, "that a belt as broad as the base of the Great Pyramid, passing round the earth, would contain one thousand millions of square feet." On his own account, he continues: —

"The height of the pyramid, casing inclusive, from base to apex, is 1-270,000th of the earth's circumference. Taking the equatorial circumference as unity, the error of this aliquot is one part in 736; but, if the polar be assumed, it is only one part in 3,506, — the former error in defect, the latter in excess. So there exists somewhere a diametral section whose circumference is exactly 270,000 times the height of the Great Pyramid. Though not a meridian, it is not very remote from one."

We believe we have indicated all the salient points of this book, — certainly all those of interest.

V.

Life and Work at the Great Pyramid in 1865, *with a Discussion of the Facts.* By C. PIAZZI SMYTH, F.R.SS.L. & E., F.R.A S., F.R.SS.A., Professor of Astronomy in the University of Edinburgh, and Astronomer-Royal for Scotland. In three vols., large octavo, 600 pp. Illustrations on Stone and Wood. Edmonston & Douglas, 1867.

THESE volumes contain the best measures of the Great Pyramid ever yet made, with plans and tables of its construction, which are probably the best that the world will ever have. We have to thank the errors of mankind for some valuable service; for the mainspring of endeavor to this man of many honors seems to have been his horror of Bunsen's rationalism, born of his theory and conviction, that the Great Pyramid was built under divine inspiration, like the tabernacle in the desert, as an ordained sample of every sort of mensuration, terrestrial and celestial! He is excessively indignant at Bunsen, for daring to suggest, that men had lived in Egypt for thousands of years before a pyramid was built; but he can only get out of the dilemma of advanced science and civilization, which Bunsen so solved, by assuming immediate divine inspiration for the builders! But the vivacious little professor is honest; and whenever his figures tell a story he does not expect, he follows them faithfully, — quite sure they will return to their allegiance by and by: and so, to do him justice, they generally do. His malignity against Bunsen is extraordinary. In those five wonderful volumes, he will never once allow for possible errors of the press: and while he points to the commanded measures of the tabernacle, corresponding to those of the Great Pyramid, and the traditions of scientific meaning attached to the latter; and raves away about the absence of every sign of idolatrous worship within it; and reminds us of the hatred the Egyptians bore its builder, because his dynasty suppressed their abominable worships, — we are certainly willing to agree with him when he plants himself on this sentence: "It cannot be wrong to attend to actual facts!" No, it cannot; and these facts are so very interesting, that, while we echo the astronomer-royal's cry to M. Renan, and exclaim, "O Smyth, Smyth! why did you not take a survey, or take photographs, *before* you founded so much history and chronology on a mechanical agreement which does not exist," yet we feel bound to bring out the salient points, and do justice to the discoveries recorded in these volumes.

The first volume is a bright, entertaining book of travels, which teaches that Arabs have the dyspepsia; that Boston thought it a "neat" thing, during the war, to prick Confederate flags into the soles of Yankee boots, which afterward tramped up and down the Pyramids in scorn, like ancient Pharaohs restored to life! It gives us a lively account of the difficulties attendant on the construction of apparatus, and the final launching of the expedition, "when, by act of Private Grace, the Secretary had procured a bag of Austrian dollars, great pancakes of things, dedicated to Maria Theresa!" — which lively sentence is a good specimen of our professor's style. The first matter of interest is his account of Mariette Bey's museum at Boolak. M. Mariette went to Egypt, some years since, in the train of the Duc de Luynes, as assistant excavator: but he showed so much talent as interpreter and explorer, that, on the departure of De Luynes, he had things his own way; and, by exhibiting his own collection, induced the authorities at Cairo to adopt it as the basis of a national museum, and was appointed "Protector to all things in and about the monuments." Renan, in writing to the "Revue des Deux Mondes," praises this museum, which "has never demolished a morsel;" and compares it with the museum at Berlin, for the creation of which the saw and hatchet were driven through the most precious things. Meanwhile Mariette Bey still seeks eagerly for inscribed stones, and with such success, that he never drives a pickaxe into a heap of rubbish without securing something of value; and De Rougé has gone back to Paris, with six large volumes of hand-copied inscriptions, which Bunsen, alas! will never see. Among his treasures are the tablet of Memphis; sculptures of the Fourth Dynasty; a greenish-black diorite, and a life-size statue of Cnephren, builder of the Great Pyramid, which is copied, for anybody who likes, in plaster. In this connection, too, we hear again of Mrs. Lieder, who did such wonders for female education in Egypt, thirty years ago; and of her husband, Dr. Lieder, to whom Bunsen gives the credit of reviving Coptic in his table, where he says, "Coptic again made intelligible in Lieder's schools, 1834." But Dr. Lieder is no more: he died of cholera while Piazzi Smyth was writing.

Scold at Bunsen as he will, our author is obliged to go to him for the meaning of the word "pyramid," which, in the new vocabulary of the fifth volume, he finds indicated,—

$P\chi\tau$, division.
Ment or *met*, the numeral X.

So here he finds a division or measure of tens, coinciding with the mechanical arrangement of a five-sided, five-cornered building, out of which his theory takes natural comfort. From the first rambling, vivacious volume, we take a few notes, before proceeding to the abstract of the scientific matter in the third. The second volume, which we take to be the valuable and lasting portion of the work, is strict measurement and mathematics, unvitiated by theory: matter, not for the critic, but for the world's scholars and speculators to use.

The Great Pyramid differs from all others in four essential particulars:—

1. The king's, or supposed sepulchral chamber, is a hundred and forty feet above ground,—a position in which no pyramid ever yet buried a man.

2. The coffer in this chamber is not built in, but stands free

upon the floor: it is too large for a coffin, and no man ever saw its lid. Sarcophagi are always sunk in the floor, and have tightly fitting lids.

3. It was expected that living men would enter and use the Great Pyramid; for its exquisitely finished ventilating tubes are a hundred and eighty feet long.

4. In pyramids for burial, the passages lead to the tomb; but the passages in the Great Pyramid apparently *lead away* from the king's chamber.

We say, apparently; but the builders left behind them a clew to the secret. In the lower part of the entrance passage, two secret key-marks, diagonal joints, carefully and expensively laid in stone, much harder than the rest, point to the triangular stone, which originally concealed the entrance to the king's chamber, and which fell so as to expose it during El Mamoom's excavation.

The pyramid is partly built of the rock itself. Pushed to the northern verge of the hill on which it stands, it is partly supported over a ravine seventy feet deep, by its own chippings worked into a solid artificial embankment. Among these chippings are splinters of green, white, and black diorite, not yet accounted for by any known remains. Easy-minded readers, having seen the account in Herodotus about the polished exterior of the pyramid, and knowing that trivial vestiges of it may still be seen, have believed what they read; but the matter has long been one of dispute, and we are glad that Piazzi Smyth's enthusiasm has settled the point for ever. He worked till he found the sockets cut in the solid rock to receive this casing; for it was necessary to find them to get the pyramid's true measure. First there was the ladder-like exterior of the masonry, then backing stones, and over them the casing, right-angled at the back and bevelled on the exterior, the angles being always of either 128° or 52°. The inside of these stones was whitish; the exterior of a bright walnut-wood brown, polished, *in situ*, beyond the power of any modern workman. At the quarries, our professor was struck with the economy of the work. There were no useless fragments; only bases of closely adjoining artificial square pillars, sliced off transversely, so that every stone measured a hundred inches in length and breadth.

Not far from a hundred feet to the south-east of the great Sphinx, our traveller went to see one of the most wonderful excavations of Mariette Bey. It is called "Shafre's tomb," and, according to Renan, "is a vast temple, different from all others known." Twenty feet below the surface, they have excavated a building a hundred and thirty feet square, with ranges of square pillars, with beams and walls of massive, polished, red granite. Limestone walls, so worn as to look like ancient cliffs, surround it. A deep pit is dug down to a portal made of three mighty granite blocks. The passage has a peculiar azimuthal angle. It emerges into a colonnaded space running north and south, having a similar arcade with a double colonnade starting from its centre, — all of red granite. A tall doorway through a granite wall looks into an *awful room*, likewise running north and south, sixty-one feet long, twelve and a half broad, and twenty high, of polished granite, with a square, sepulchral well pierced through a floor of brilliant crystalline alabaster, near the middle of its east side. Here Cnephren's statue was found, a hundred and seventy-five inches below the surface, — under water, in fact, — with many other broken things rudely hurled in, as if an enemy had done it. The granite which built these polished walls was brought six hundred miles for the purpose.

Our author went to see this newly discovered building, as a sort of recreation in the midst of his hard work. When he returns, he describes to us four sets of grooves in the antechamber of the Great Pyramid, in which it has been supposed that four stone portcullises once ran up and down. Our author shakes his head over this; for though three pairs are really grooves, reaching from ceiling to floor, the fourth still holds what has been happily called a "granite leaf;" and this is no portcullis. It is cemented into the south groove, but is twenty inches from the north wall. The groove reaches only as far as the leaf falls; so that this never could have descended lower, and, if it had, it would only partly bar the passage, being but one third its height. This leaf is formed of two stones, one above the other, cemented together with the most precious white cement, the upper with a sort of semicircular bevelled handle, which looks as if it were made to draw the leaf upward in the grooves, and so disclose a secret. This is all our professor knows, and he leaves his reader as excited as himself over the evident mystery.

Professor Smyth is greatly astonished at the justness of the pyramid's orientation. Nouet, in 1799, made it nineteen minutes of an arc out; but, in 1865, Smyth finds the error only four minutes and a few seconds, and this he thinks was not an error, but intentional, as it is the same in the second pyramid. No man's instrumental work, not even the famous Troughton's, is perfect; but it was very surprising, that the amount of difference between the *two halves* of Troughton's azimuth circle was greater than the angular difference between the azimuthal directions of axes in the Great Pyramid and the second pyramid, so very nearly had the ancient builders made two difficult things exactly alike. At this moment, the well-chamber in " King Shafre's tomb " gives a better observation of the instant of noon, than all the " time-finding means in Cairo." It gave a feeling almost of awe, to discover the same accuracy in the sockets of the casing cut in the rock: no socket " sights " the other precisely; but what small error there is, is plainly accounted for by piles of intervening rubbish.

At the very opening of volume third, in which we are to encounter a charming medley of "fact and fiction," our professor quotes, from Hekekyan Bey's " Chronology of Siriadic Monuments," a passage which we commend to all critics of Bunsen, and himself in particular: —

> " But we must be on our guard not to assign the construction of a monument, in all cases, to the monarch whose name is most prominently legible on it. There was a colossal statue, of largest size, in Memphis, the cylinders of which had been so diminished by cutting down for new cartouches to be engraved, that a mortise was made through and through each hand for the insertion of new cylinders. Standard statues, of the size of life, had hollows in their faces for the introduction of features resembling those of the reigning king!"

In Hekekyan Bey our readers will recognize a prominent friend of European influence, and especially of Dr. Lieder and female education in Egypt.

Postponing for the moment such peculiar notions as Professor Smyth may entertain, we wish to draw attention to some remarkable traits in the construction of the Great Pyramid, now for the first time distinctly brought out, and of great value to all theorists, sane and insane.

1. The angle of the sides of the Great Pyramid is of precisely the amount to cause the linear proportion which twice the length of one of its sides bears to the vertical height of the whole mass, to be that of the diameter to the circle, — the constant quantity π of all modern mathematics.

2. Three trenches, which observers have always insisted were used solely for the mixing of mortar, gave Professor Smyth the feeling from the beginning, that they had to do with deciding the dominant angles of the pyramid; and from his observation he proves them to be *azimuth trenches*, their mean determination being 51° 51' 33". These trenches, then, were placed at the actual angles intentionally or unintentionally. If the former, the builders knew what remarkable property they could give to a pyramid, by constructing its slope at the critical angle of 51° 51'; " and we shall do wisely to attend with care to their other angular works." Why did not this consideration save you, O Professor! from the theory of divine inspiration and its consequences?

3. In its descending passage, the Great Pyramid is like all others; but in the ascending, indicated by the diagonals, it is unique. Of the three passages, we ought to know the inclination; but to compare the Grand Gallery with the celestial polar direction we must bore through the blocks of stone, with which it is still choked! The pyramid shows only one of the two daily meridian transits of a pole-star particularly marked, yet accounts for, or shows the direction of, the other transit, and the place of the pole as well.

4. The Great Pyramid stands ninety miles from the Red Sea, and a hundred and ten in a direct line from the Mediterranean. Its correct orientation has always been taken for granted; and we have shown how small, and perhaps intentional, our professor found the error. As regards latitude, the theoretical angle is 30°; what Piazzi Smyth actually found is 29° 58' 51". Why did not the builders hit the mark a little more closely, carry it 69" farther north, and make it perfectly accurate? The answer to this question he finds in the topography of the region. To have carried it even this little to the north, would have taken it off a noble hill, and buried it ingloriously in a broad bay of sand. By pushing it to the extreme northern end of the cliff, — where one landslip had already occurred, and which they were compelled to fill up with good masonry, — they showed that they knew their error.

5. A system of inclined passages in the rock north-east of the pyramid, about which there has been a good deal of speculation, our astronomer considers merely a model on which the masons tried their hand, to work out the *internal figures* of the pyramid, as the azimuth trenches had worked out the external angles. That part of the actual pyramid which was cut in the rock has

suffered more from time than that part which is made of masonry. As to any changes produced by time, six different subjects of observation, including the geological strata, combine to show a southward dip. It is only about 32″, however, — hardly worth noting. A shining, curly, white, moss-like excrescence, appearing in the Grand Gallery and queen's chamber, proves to be common salt.

6. Taylor taught us to look at the internal axis of the earth's rotation, which he estimated at five hundred millions of inches, for the builder's measure, — this statement being defended and enforced by Sir John Herschel. Taylor took Newton's sacred cubit, a measure always employed by the Hebrews for sacred purposes, — twenty-five inches long. The modern French metre was chosen as the one ten-millionth of a quadrant of a particular meridian of the earth. The sacred cubit was the one ten-millionth of half the earth's axis of rotation, — also a useful measure, close on the length of the human arm and the human pace; and of these cubits there are as many contained *in one side of the pyramid's base*, as there are days in the year! Here is the pyramid linear measure: —

1 thumb-breadth,	= 1 inch.
1 arm, roughly,	= 1 cubit, or 25 inches.
100 acre-sides,	= 1 acre-side.
25 acre-sides,	= 1 mile.
100 cubits,	= 1 league.

The cubic contents of the great coffer have been elsewhere shown to be equal to one Hebrew laver, or one English chaldron. Now for the measure of weight. A cubic measure being formed, with sides of a ten-millionth of the earth's axis of rotation, a tenth part of this space is to be filled with matter of the specific density of the earth. This mass will form the weight standard. The coffer measure puts the mean density at 5.70.

7. Decimal measures are every where indicated, and show the coffer to be *intentionally* what it is, thinks our professor. Four vertical grooves divide the entrance wall of the king's chamber into five parts. The coffer, whose capacity is also that ascribed to the Ark of the Covenant, is founded on a fifty-inch measure, the one ten-millionth of the earth's axis of rotation. It stands in a room carefully divided by five equal courses of stone; a thing not to be done in that hard material without extreme care. By the position of the floor on the lower course, the room becomes a

measure of the same capacity as Solomon's molten sea, fifty times that of the coffer, — fifty and five are the ruling numbers. Then again the king's chamber holds an unexpected relation to the whole pyramid. The fiftieth course of stone in the pyramid is identical with the floor of that chamber. On it stands the coffer of fifty inches standard, in its tank of fifty times itself, with walls of five courses; and, if that coffer's contents of water be divided by fifty times fifty, we get the pyramid pound, scientifically checked all the world over as five cubic inches of the earth's mean density! We agree with our professor, that, if this is all accurate and all accidental, it is very bewildering.

He goes on to show that the ventilators were constructed so as to create a mean temperature of what he calls *one-fifth*.

Now, whereas the king's chamber has a relation to a measure of fives and fifties, so the queen's chamber has a similar relation to a standard of twenty-five; and the subterranean chamber was equally a chamber of angular measure. By calculations concerning the latter, which our readers would not care to follow, our professor gets a compass with divisions of *fives*, which he thinks the sailors would be grateful for! In the seven-sided crystalline form of the queen's chamber, his peculiar notions lead him to find an index of the sabbatical week; and he somewhere quotes our much-maligned Bunsen in his own support. If figures were ever "off on a strike," we think they would have refused to contribute to such a result.

The third volume contains an interesting but contemptuous account of the labors of Mahmoud Bey, alluded to in our article on Bunsen. It seems to trouble our astronomer a good deal, that he cannot criticise the excellence of Mahmoud's mathematical work.

In his speculative advances, Smyth makes a queer choice of authorities; and, whenever he brings up a peculiarly obscure name, he shows his real respect for Bunsen, by reporting what good thing the baron credited to it! If a third of the time spent on the building of this pyramid was spent, as Herodotus says, in subterranean work, then our professor is sure that we shall yet see the inside of an undiscovered chamber, in which will be works of the magnificent diorite, whose splinters strike through the embankment. No man knows where this diorite came from; no one has ever reported it *in situ*.

Professor Smyth treats us, in closing, to Haliburton's "Essay on the Pleiades." All nations, he thinks, once had a year of pleiads, before the rise of the great heathen civilizations, and in which is the explanation of the old festival of Hallowe'en. This year began with the autumnal equinox, "the mother-night of the year." But, for all this, he must needs borrow of Bunsen the very star-maps and charts Professor Heiss prepared for him! One thing he has decided, — that the Dog-star shall not rule the pyramid. Those who know what good work is, however, will always value Professor Smyth's second volume, and turn from his third to Bunsen's noble five, with ever-fresh delight.

THE END.

www.ingramcontent.com/pod-product-compliance
Lightning Source LLC
Chambersburg PA
CBHW020124170426
43199CB00009B/629